T0343520

Lessons from
My Teachers

Lessons from My Teachers

From Preschool to the Present

Sarah Ruhl

MARYSUE
RUCCI
BOOKS

New York   Amsterdam/Antwerp   London
Toronto   Sydney/Melbourne   New Delhi

MARYSUE RUCCI BOOKS

An Imprint of Simon & Schuster, LLC
1230 Avenue of the Americas
New York, NY 10020

For more than 100 years, Simon & Schuster has championed authors and the stories they create. By respecting the copyright of an author's intellectual property, you enable Simon & Schuster and the author to continue publishing exceptional books for years to come. We thank you for supporting the author's copyright by purchasing an authorized edition of this book.

First Marysue Rucci Books hardcover edition May 2025

MARYSUE RUCCI BOOKS and colophon are trademarks of Simon & Schuster, LLC

Simon & Schuster strongly believes in freedom of expression and stands against censorship in all its forms. For more information, visit BooksBelong.com.

For information about special discounts for bulk purchases, please contact Simon & Schuster Special Sales at 1-866-506-1949 or business@simonandschuster.com.

The Simon & Schuster Speakers Bureau can bring authors to your live event. For more information or to book an event, contact the Simon & Schuster Speakers Bureau at 1-866-248-3049 or visit our website at www.simonspeakers.com.

Interior design by Laura Levatino

Manufactured in the United States of America

10 9 8 7 6 5 4 3 2 1

Library of Congress Control Number: 2024055256

ISBN 978-1-6680-3496-5
ISBN 978-1-6680-3498-9 (ebook)

For all my teachers—
especially for Kathy Ruhl and Paula Vogel.
And in memory of Tina Howe and Joyce Piven.

The relation in education is one of true dialogue.

—Martin Buber

A teacher comes, they say, when you are ready. And if you ignore its presence, it will speak to you more loudly. But you have to be quiet to hear.

—Robin Wall Kimmerer, *Braiding Sweetgrass: Indigenous Wisdom, Scientific Knowledge, and the Teachings of Plants*

Contents

Introduction   1

One. *Roots*

1. For my first teacher, my mother   7
2. Lessons from preschool   11
3. *All I Really Need to Know I Learned in Kindergarten* redux   14
4. The elementary school art teacher who gave an assignment I hated   19
5. Mr. Spangenberger and enduring rejection   20
6. The principal who once seemed fearsome   23
7. Sunday school teachers and bullies   26
8. Sisterhood is powerful   29
9. When middle C is not the middle   31
10. The perfect bookstore   34
11. Joyce Piven, and how to listen   37
12. Rilke and the romance of solitude   42
13. My father and words as nourishment   46
14. Paula Vogel   51
15. Ancient Tragedy and Its Influence   56
16. Big questions   59
17. There has been a death in the family   61
18. How to drop out of graduate school   65
19. Tina Howe and the pink elephant   68

20. See one, do one, teach one 73
21. Gifts 77
22. María Irene Fornés on pleasure and the moment 79

Two. *Branches*

23. Lessons from a marriage 85
24. Beth Henley and luck 91
25. Dr. Seuss and Virginia Woolf, or letter to my daughters 93
26. A lesson from Hope 98
27. Learning to swim 101
28. Why aren't you cheering for my sister?
    Or: the headless gerbils 103
29. How to leave a meeting with a monster 105
30. Ezra the falafel maker 107
31. Lessons from critics 108
32. Gloria Steinem 112
33. Stage fright and mothers and daughters 116
34. My daughter on dramatic irony and death 119
35. When your babysitter is also your dharma teacher 121
36. Walking a dog, or a toddler 128
37. Giving your kids your divided attention 130
38. Lessons from bleeding 132

Three. *Flowers*

39. Anne and the natural world as teacher 137
40. On Shabbat 141
41. The gardener 144
42. My dog knows everything 147
43. Max, or learning from your student 149

44. Lesson on an Amtrak train from a monk   153

45. When your shrink is also your dharma teacher   156

46. The healing power of literature   158

47. The show must not go on   164

48. Learning from Scheherazade
    while binge-watching *Succession*   168

49. Penelope, weaving and revising   171

50. Lesson from a cranky neighbor   174

51. Arthur Miller and Tony Kushner are tall   176

52. The sad neighbor   179

53. Polly and the two-dollar-bill dream   181

54. On writer's block   183

55. A practical use of meditation   190

56. Theater as a school of presence   193

57. Can you be your own teacher?   197

58. My mother and Peter Pan   203

59. Becoming a teacher   208

60. Epilogue, or how I wrote this book   213

Acknowledgments   217

Lessons from
My Teachers

Introduction

I teach a playwriting class at Yale called Lessons from My Teachers. I created the course because I wanted to remind my students that there is no one way to learn how to write a play. I also wanted to honor my own teachers, to pass on what they taught me to the next generation. In the class, I teach the students not only the plays my own teachers wrote, but I also try to teach *the way* they taught. I want my students to know that playwrights are made, not born—and they're made from a web of affiliation and lineage, rather than springing from the head of Zeus, original and complete. But perhaps I also created the class because I missed my own teachers and wanted to continue to learn from them, by teaching their work again and again.

I went through a dark period in which the world seemed to have shrunk. The world seemed to be the size of my pocket, in which was a phone. I felt pulled toward my phone, as if to a magnet, staring at it like an oracle, as though my phone could answer all kinds of spiritual, political, literary, medical, and practical questions. I doomscrolled—extreme weather and extreme politics. Then a pandemic, bodily symptoms, child-rearing, war . . . But I found few answers on my phone, only very loud opinions. I longed for my own teachers—the human ones, not the ones on my screen.

When my son, William, was little, I often found him borrowing my phone to look up all kinds of arcane questions: *How fast can a cheetah run? How do you make a cream puff? Is Oobleck a liquid or a solid? How do you build an igloo?* Then, when he was eight years old, I observed him asking my phone what the meaning of life was.

Siri: What is the meaning of life? he asked.

The phone told him there was no consensus.

Oh dear, I thought. *This is a crisis.*

My children needed my wisdom. So did my students. And where was I? In my own pocket, in the dark. My teachers, some of them, were dying. A dear student, Max Ritvo, had died at the age of twenty-five. My mother was getting older. My children were still little, and I was care-taking in two directions. My health kept falling apart, mysteriously. I was full of spiritual longing. I was also exhausted. I'd had some tough knocks from critics. I wasn't in the mood to write a new play. I felt re-active, on edge. Angry that my body was betraying me with strange symptoms, angry that the world was on fire. And I was supposed to be the teacher now. A grown-up, with answers. And yet, I had so many questions.

At night, I'd lie in bed in a stupor, searching the opinion pages on a bright little screen. I asked questions about our fragile democracy, how to cook a chicken, what it meant that I had a strange burning sensation in my ear. That the questions were all directed toward a screen gave the answers a flattening sameness. When I made my phone grayscale to dis-tance myself from the pull of information, I felt slightly less compelled, and then I thought, *Am I addicted to the color of information and not infor-mation itself? And what of wisdom? What color is it?*

I wanted to transmit wisdom and optimism to my students when I myself wanted to know how to keep going in the sometimes-brutal field of "show business," which, during the pandemic, was the nonexistent field of show business. I also wanted to give optimism and wisdom to my children, when sometimes it felt as though my roots had been pulled up and were fraying around my knees.

I felt dimly that I needed my own teacher to teach me all the things my phone would never teach me. I knew that my phone could not teach me how to love, how to work, or, perhaps more important, how to *keep* working. I would make lists of "Things My Phone Can't Teach Me": How to love. How to mourn. How to be quiet. Et cetera. And yet I continued to consult the tiny rectangular oracle at night. I clicked on tabs; they would say: "Confirm your humanity." I would notice on Wordle that the word *ANGER* became the word *ANGEL* with just one letter substitution. *How do I turn the R to the L?* I would think. And then the phrase "the better angels of our nature" came to me, and I would wonder: *Who said that?* Again, my phone told me. Abraham Lincoln did, when he was trying to unite the Union. But knowing that information did not help me sleep better as I watched our fragile democracy seem to eat itself.

In the daylight, I wanted to return to my roots for ballast and support—to the real, human lessons my teachers had already taught me. I wanted their voices in my head. That I've absorbed guidance from all kinds of *real* people and places seems an obvious thing to say, and yet, one irony of our digital era, in which we desperately try to learn from YouTube, is that our phones can give us facts but not story; information, but not *relation*. And yet I believe passionately that one of the main lessons teachers can give is their singular presence—the nimble strength of connection. The great teachers are often those whose teaching cannot be done to scale, whose lessons depend on specificity of place, time, and relationship.

In other words—a teaching that is truly absorbed is composed not of words only but also of the *example* of the person doing the teaching. A lesson received is often a *how* rather than a *what* because the word is passed through an embodied person—more relation than idiom; more connection than mnemonic device. The teachers who have most affected me have modeled how to be *in relationship* rather than simply transmitting reducible content to me.

And so, this is a book about many of the teachers I was lucky enough to have had over the course of my life. It is, in a way, a portrait of my life told through portraits of my teachers. Sometimes I found my teachers in a classroom proper, other times in books, dreams, the natural world, neighbors, friends, children, and in the theater.

I hope to continue to orient myself as a student in this world. The more I teach, the more I learn, and the more I see teachers all around me. I'm grateful for the process of writing this book, because it led me back to my teachers, and I dedicate it to all of them, living and dead.

One

Roots

Does the wind move the trees
or do the trees move the wind?
A child might ask, or God.

For my first teacher, my mother

My mother was a teacher. She taught English. As it happens, she was also my first teacher.

When I was a child, my mother always seemed busy, in the *midst*, in the great flow of life. She was grading English papers written by the young scholars at Regina Dominican high school. Or she was in a play, or gardening, driving, reading, smoking, sewing. She wrote down stories for me as I composed them, before I could even write. She taught me what a Venn diagram was. She taught me how to diagram a sentence. She taught me the lyrics to every Rodgers and Hammerstein musical. She *tried* to teach me how to knit, but the craft gene skipped over me entirely. She always seemed to take pleasure in the tasks before her—warm, and in motion.

Anyone who knows my mother knows her as a charismatic force, who has just read *the most interesting book*, can talk to even the most reluctant talker and get their life story out of them.

But ten years ago, my mother called me on the phone sounding sad, and I said, "How are you?"

She said, "Okay."

I heard a hesitation in her voice and asked, "Why only okay?"

And she said, "Well, I'm still having trouble with a sense of what my mission is in life."

When that call came, my mom was in her seventh decade, and I was in my fourth. But we've been having this conversation since I was about ten years old, in some form or another.

"I don't have a legacy," she said on the phone.

I asked her if it was not enough that she had two daughters, one who wrote plays and one who was a doctor. "Does that count as a legacy?" I asked.

"Not really," she said. "That is not mine. It's yours. Maybe"—she sighed—"I didn't plan enough."

My mother grew up in the fifties. The feminist movement came along just as she was moving to the suburbs and having babies. She did not plan a career arc, to get to place x by age y. She was not part of any consciousness-raising groups; she did not look at her vagina while standing over mirrors. She made us brown-bag lunches, on which she'd make little drawings, anagrams, a small crossword puzzle of my name. She read us *Mrs. Piggle-Wiggle* and did all the funny voices. She took our temperatures, made us chicken soup and baked potatoes. She knitted us sweaters and recited the words of absurdist playwrights, like Ionesco. She made us laugh. She volunteered at school, directed the third-grade play. I asked her once why she volunteered at my elementary school to direct plays, and she told me it wasn't done out of charity; she did it because she was bored, and she wanted to make theater.

My mother is a thinker. She's worried that death will be without thinking, without consciousness; she's terrified by the idea that we leave it all behind. If consciousness persisted somehow, would there still be something she wished that she had *done*? And what would that thing be? I felt some guilt. Had my mother given up her ambitions to raise me and my sister? After I gave birth to my first baby, Anna, my mother came to help for two weeks. I remember being depleted from breastfeeding, and how good it tasted to eat a simple breakfast of toast with smashed-up hard-boiled egg that my mother had made me. It was as though, in order to make food for my baby, I needed my mother to make food for me. As my mother was leaving, getting into the taxi for the airport, she called, "Remember, don't feel guilty if you resent the baby!" *Ah,* I thought.

My mother was always acting in some play or other at the North Shore community theater during my childhood, and I would come with her to small, darkened theaters, sitting in the back, taking notes, which she would sometimes pass on to the director. I learned the magic of the theater sitting in the dark and watching her act. How many plays has she been in? Over a hundred at least. And why, in her mind, does it not add up to a mission? All these vivid characters—Joan of Arc, Peter Pan, Dull Gret, Mrs. Fezziwig—all these women and boys she's inhabited for the sheer pleasure of doing it. And now I wonder, why do all the roles she played not feel to her as though she left something behind? Is theater too transient? But what is permanent? Words? Works? Children? Education? How many young women has she educated? She poured Dickens and the *Odyssey* into the minds of young women. She worked hard for her PhD in her fifties, scaling the theoreticians while we were all bowled over with grief after my father's early death. Does that count? Does making sure her daughters grew up solid after that loss count? Would fame count? Everything perishes eventually, it's only a matter of degrees.

What if our mission was, as the critic Walter Pater puts it, "not to sleep before evening"? He wrote, in the nineteenth century, "Every moment some form grows perfect in hand or face; some tone on the hills or the sea is choicer than the rest; some mood of passion or insight or intellectual excitement is irresistibly real and attractive to us—for that moment only. Not the fruit of experience, but experience itself, is the end. Not to discriminate every moment some passionate attitude in those about us . . . is to sleep before evening."

My mother has lived by Pater's injunction to be fully in the present moment her whole life. If I had to choose between all the lessons she has taught me and hold one holy, it is this—to live in the moment. Virginia Woolf was the literary master of catching the moment as it floats by, and she once wrote that "a woman writing thinks back through her mothers." Woolf was very exacting with her punctuation and her spelling, and she said *mothers*, plural. Not just your own mother. Did Woolf mean our literary mothers, whom we have in abundance? Or did she mean our biological mothers and *their* mothers? Or did she mean, in the Buddhist sense (a stretch for Woolf) that we've all been reincarnated countless times and that we've all had many mothers?

There is a Tibetan Buddhist prayer in which you think closely about your mother. You imagine all the impossible tasks she did for you, the ways in which she suffered for you, all the care and compassion she gave to keep you alive. You then, in your own mind, offer your mother all your happiness, and take all of her suffering for yourself.

I have a wish that my mother will, someday, feel that she's accomplished enough. That she will know in her bones that her teachings found fertile ground, that she can claim all that she taught, to her students, and to me.

That she will look around this earth and say, *Yes, it was good.*

Lessons from preschool

The first thing I remember about preschool is saying goodbye to my mother. I didn't want to be separated from her, and I clung to her legs when she dropped me off at the basement of St. Francis Xavier Catholic Church, where my family went on Christmas and Easter. I cried for my mother. I stayed at the bottom of the dark staircase and looked up for the light, and for her.

The teacher, Mrs. Anne, gently led me by the hand to the big open room. Around me, kids were doing Montessori-type activities, counting strings of beads in the bead center and making inkblots out of potatoes. Gentle, slim, tall Mrs. Anne wore beige slacks and reapplied light pink lipstick in a mirror when she thought we weren't looking. She led us through circle time, but mostly we were left to our own devices. We washed dishes in soapy water, looked at light through a prism. Eventually, I learned to love the quiet and calm of the classroom. While I was concentrating, I was learning; and while I was learning, I did not miss my mother.

Is all of school a way of saying goodbye to your parents to make room for other teachers in life? Is the beginning of school a way of saying your parents can't teach you everything, and you need independence of mind to go on your way through the world?

Years later, when I was searching for a preschool for my first daughter, I started reading the philosophy of Maria Montessori and was charmed by her thinking, quite radical in her day. Her classrooms were child-centered—a new philosophical approach in the hierarchical world of children's education at the turn of the twentieth century. Montessori deeply respected children's minds and cultivated their independence.

She designed the classroom so that chairs were child-size, and students could freely explore rather than learning by rote. Montessori wrote: "The child who concentrates is immensely happy."

No wonder so many children and adults are miserable today in our age of distraction. *"The child who concentrates is immensely happy."* When I think back on the joyful, calm, focused attention of that preschool church basement, I realize I learned very early a preference for solitary activity and quiet while I was working.

I taught myself to read in that church basement. Reading was a portal into a private world away from other children. By the time I was four, I could read many books, including the Dick and Jane books and my beloved Fat Albert book, which I found at preschool and coveted. I *loved* that Fat Albert book and wanted to make it mine.

One day in preschool, leaving the church, I stole it. I stole that Fat Albert book. I put it under my shirt and walked right out of the basement. Out of a *church* basement! It was a sin, that much I knew. Why did I love that book so much I wanted to possess it? Maybe I was amazed by the fact that the characters I watched at home on television had made their way onto the pages of a book. The characters were vivid to me; they felt like my own friends. I'm not sure why I didn't ask to *borrow* the book, why I felt I had to *possess* it.

At any rate, by the time I had successfully sneaked *The Wit and Wisdom of Fat Albert* home under my shirt and gotten away with it, I felt so guilty that I cried and then threw the book in the garbage. I feared if I left it out in plain sight I would be punished. At Sunday school, also at St. Francis, I had learned that stealing was a sin. Now, not only had I deprived myself of the book, as it was in the garbage, but I had also deprived all the other children at school of the book!

Stealing a book and feeling guilty about it is one of my earliest memories—is it any wonder I became a writer? Aren't we taught that artists must steal? T. S. Eliot once said, "Immature poets imitate; mature poets steal; bad poets deface what they take, and good poets make it into something better or at least something different." I teach my own students not to steal but to transform; to metamorphosize the ideas of the ancients rather than stealing from one's contemporaries.

Perhaps I learned at an early age that once you learn to read, you might love the work of others so much that you might be driven to steal, but it's better to leave that work in the common space, for the whole community, and not to hoard.

Another lesson I learned: if I got separated from my mother, the classroom would hold me.

All I Really Need to Know I Learned in Kindergarten *redux*

I always found it terrifying in the fall, when I was a new student, to perform before I knew if the teacher liked me. I loved school, dreaded summer, and wanted to please my teachers. When summer did come, and the rest of the kids welcomed free time joyfully, I comforted myself by playing school. It occurred to me, when I became a teacher, that not every student had the same relationship to school. I wanted to find out how my students felt about their own kindergarten memories so that I could learn how they might see the position of teacher.

Though the word *school* has mostly connotations of learning and safety for me, I knew that it might not have the same connotations for my students. I passionately did not want to reproduce conditions of unfairness or a model of authoritarian leadership. My graduate students were in their twenties or thirties, with a variety of life experiences in terms of geography, ethnicity, and class. And as they walked into the Gothic edifice that is Yale to make vulnerable, groundbreaking art, I wanted to know how they viewed early experiences of school. For some students, the word *teacher* might have positive connotations, while the word *school* might not. I wanted to know: How could I be a teacher but not a wielder of hierarchical structures?

One fall, after I'd been teaching graduate playwriting students for six years, I started out the semester by reading them excerpts of *All I Really Need to Know I Learned in Kindergarten* by Robert Fulghum. Fulghum extracts credos from his own kindergarten experience and applies them to life more broadly: "Share everything. Play fair. Put things back where you found them. Clean up your own mess." He concludes that if only international corporations, world governments, and billionaire families had followed such dictums, we would be living in a different kind of place, from climate change to poverty. Fulghum, a white Unitarian minister from Texas, talks about these precepts as though they are universal; I wasn't sure if my students would see it that way.

I asked my students to write their own lists of "All I really need to know I learned in kindergarten." While I waited for my students to write their lists, I wrote my own list, channeling my inner five-year-old:

- Kids can be cruel; that is why we need grown-ups around on the playground.
- Anders Wick, who sits in front of me, is from Norway, and in Norway they have real candles on their trees at Christmas.
- Grown-ups make me feel safe among children who are unpredictable.
- When your mother appears in the middle of the school day to pick you up, it is because someone has died. (My father's mother died when I was in first grade, and my mother came to pick me up in the middle of the school day.)
- Don't run down long hallways just because you feel like running, that will get you in trouble. In time you will forget what it feels like to have enough energy that you feel like running for no reason. But by that time, you will have learned that it is socially unacceptable.
- Books are safe.
- My teacher tells my mother I have a large vocabulary but I don't know what the word *vocabulary* means. Not knowing what *vocabulary* means when you are told you have a large one is how it feels to be five.
- It feels wonderful if another girl plays with your hair while you are sitting on the rug during story time but this can get you in trouble.

After we'd all written our lists, we shared them out loud. The lists of my students had some kindergarten experiences that bore similarities to Fulghum's, and many other lessons specific to their own life experiences. Some of my students wrote rosy dictums about what they learned in kindergarten; others learned that institutions can be punishing, restrictive, and often unfair, and that on top of institutions being unfair, life itself is not fair. Still others learned that they hated sitting on a chair and not moving all day, and for two of them, it was alienating to be speaking English at school when English was their second language. "English is a fundamentally dishonest language" was a lesson learned from a playwright who grew up speaking Korean in his home.

After reading our individual lists, we wrote collective lists, moving from "Things I Learned in Kindergarten" to "Things *We* Learned in Kindergarten." These are the dictums we felt we could keep for our graduate school classroom:

Things We Learned in Kindergarten

- Go outside in the sun.
- I am enough.
- Your classmates are your friends.
- Sometimes you can feel lonely in a group.
- Routine helps.
- Erasers exist because we make mistakes.
- English is hard.
- Know your history.
- Take naps.
- Snacks are good.
- My mom won't always be there, and then I feel alone.

- Imaginary friends are okay.
- Treat others as you would like to be treated.
- If you don't have anything nice to say, don't say anything at all.
- Say I'm sorry.
- Forgive.
- Don't pee in the sandbox.
- Share.
- Use your words.
- Use your manners.
- Take turns.
- Be on time.
- Say please and thank you.
- Color everything.
- Respect your elders.
- Don't exclude people even if you don't like them.
- Don't interrupt.
- If you ask to copy people's drawings they will be flattered, but if you don't ask they will be annoyed.
- Be helpful.
- Hug people when they return.
- Conflict can be healthy.
- Learn how to make friends.
- Learn how to play.
- Learn how to be quiet.
- Learn how to sing.
- Learn how to get everyone to imagine what I'm imagining.
- Know how much I already know myself.
- Story time should come before nap time.
- Listen.
- It's okay to miss your mom.
- Don't break what you're working on.

- Stories are everywhere here.
- Stay in the group.
- Everyone's embarrassed and also not embarrassed.
- You can mess things up quickly, but cleaning up a mess takes a long time. Still, it's okay to make a mess.
- Things take time.
- Don't hit me.
- Story time is sacred.

The elementary school art teacher who gave an assignment I hated

"*Don't pound the paper!*" Mr. P, our elementary school art teacher used to shout at us. He was a terrifying man. And he did not make art fun.

I remember vividly one assignment he gave us in third grade: he told us to draw something colorful, in crayon. I set to work. I loved what I made—a landscape, with vibrant swathes of color. Then he told us to paint black all over it. I was horrified. He wanted us to paint over our crayon drawings, then take a pin and etch designs into the paint to reveal abstract color patterns underneath.

I refused. I loved my crayon drawing. I was quietly defiant. I thought his assignment was stupid. But he came over to my shoulder, saw that I wasn't working, and shouted at me to paint over my drawing. He might even have painted over it himself with black paint, then handed me a pin to make designs. I never forgave him. I hated the new abstract work of art, with the little pin lines of color showing through. I wanted my original artwork back.

Years later, my sister and I were cleaning out a bureau at my mother's when she was moving, and we found a little misshapen ceramic chicken my sister had made in elementary school. We looked at the bottom of her ceramic chicken where she had scrawled her name, along with this sentence: "I hate Mr. P."

What lesson did I draw from this experience?

Sometimes the teacher is wrong, and you should refuse to do their assignment.

Mr. Spangenberger and enduring rejection

Mr. Spangenberger was my fourth-grade teacher at Central Elementary School in Wilmette, Illinois. Lanky and blue-eyed, with a duck-like shock of yellow hair atop his head, he was missing half of his ring finger on one hand. He told us that the missing digit was a result of a canoe trip he took; he said he'd dangled his hand in the water and a piranha bit off his finger. The kids all believed this religiously, but now I'm not so sure.

If we behaved ourselves, Mr. Spangenberger would reward us by playing his guitar and singing for us. How we loved hearing him play and sing "Blue Suede Shoes" or "Johnny B. Goode."

We studied landmasses in science that year. I took it upon myself to write a play, my first full-length: a courtroom drama about an isthmus. All the landmasses spoke—islands, archipelagoes, mountains. The dispute between landmasses in my play got heated. And the sun had to come down and settle things, a deus ex machina.

I still have the landmass play, handwritten and saved in a groovy pink- and blue-flowered binder. It began like this:

SKY: I watch the earth from above.
WATER: I watch the earth while traveling.
LAND: I watch the earth on a level.
SKY: As I watch there has been a shortage in the water system.
LAND: That is very true. The tributary has stopped functioning and there has been confusion ever since.

This would have been 1986, before discussions about climate change had entered elementary schools. I'm not sure what possessed me. I gave

Mr. Spangenberger the play, hopeful that he would produce it in the big auditorium. He said no.

I learned my first lesson as a playwright: after your first rejection, keep writing. I went on to write many plays and, oddly, even a play—*Eurydice*—with a chorus of talking stones. When I met my teacher, the playwright Paula Vogel (you will hear more about her later), she would give the most wonderful sermons on rejection, inoculating her students against future disappointments.

Paula would say: "Listen. There are four kinds of rejection letters from theaters."

This was back when we sent physical scripts through the postal service and got back actual rejection letters in the mail.

Paula went on to anatomize each variety of rejection: "The first kind of rejection letter is xeroxed—an unsigned pro forma letter saying, basically, please don't send us any more plays."

I got plenty of those early on. I remember one xeroxed rejection letter from a theater in Texas, about my play *Melancholy Play*, in which a woman becomes so sad she turns into an almond. The letter said something to the effect of: *We do experimental work like the work of Suzan-Lori Parks. Your play is not experimental. Please don't send us any plays ever again.* I was particularly disappointed because I loved the work of Suzan-Lori Parks.

Paula would go on to say, "The second kind of rejection letter is a real *signed* letter from someone in the literary office. This means that your play made it through an army of interns and was read by the literary manager. It's *signed*. Lick your finger and test the ink. That means you are in a special pile."

I would test the ink of these rejection letters and feel exalted that I'd made it through the interns. One memorable letter of this category, also about *Melancholy Play*, said, "We don't even think your play is a play." But it was *signed*.

The next category, Paula went on to describe, was "a signed letter saying they *loved* your play, though they can't produce it, but please send the *next play.* They don't ask everyone to send another play, believe me," Paula said. This was a letter to keep, and to follow instructions—send the next play.

The final category of rejection letter goes something like, "We loved your new play, but it's not for us; still, if you're in town, could you come in and meet with us at some point?" Paula said this rejection letter was *very rare*—a rejection along with a bid for an in-person meeting—this was only about 3 percent of rejection letters. It made me feel very fancy and special when I received my first "let's meet up" rejection letter. Rather than feeling dejected, I called the literary manager who had signed the letter—Lisa McNulty—then the literary manager at the Women's Project Theater in New York City. I'll never forget meeting her for the first time. She had on a leopard-print miniskirt and high Doc Martens, and we made friends immediately. She would go on to many other jobs in the theater, finally landing back at the Women's Project, this time as artistic director, where she would go on to produce one of my plays—*Dear Elizabeth*—twenty or so years later.

And so: you never know where rejection might lead. Sometimes a rejection leads you to your next collaborator, your next friend, your next play. Not that I would counsel anyone to make a fetish out of rejection letters, as my friend the writer Jacob Appel did, wallpapering his Morningside Heights apartment with all of his rejection letters, until his living room resembled a masochistic literary version of stuffed tigers on the wall.

In the case of Mr. Spangenberger, the rejection of the landmass play led me to switching genres for a while, turning to poems and short stories, for which I needed no producer. Every rejection contains a possibility for tacking into the wind. The main thing is to persist.

I'm still looking for a producer of that courtroom drama about talking landmasses. It couldn't be more topical now—when the land is literally speaking to us, screaming at us, really, to pay attention.

The principal who once seemed fearsome

In fifth grade, I was called into the principal's office after a food fight in the cafeteria. I was an irritatingly well-behaved child. I was writing a novella about a mischievous young boy named Corey who would get into trouble for his rule-breaking adventures, but I ran out of ideas, possibly because I never broke school rules. So, when I was called into the principal's office for the first time, it was a shock.

A boy named F. J. Phillips had thrown a french fry at me at a long table in a massive food fight. I threw the french fry back at him. The cafeteria lady spotted me and pointed. I was walked down the green-tiled hallway with the other perps to the office. Principal Nilsen started his interrogation with me. I was terrified.

"Did you throw food at the food fight?" he asked in a deep intimidating voice.

"Yes," I said tremulously. "But it was only one french fry—"

"I didn't ask *what* you threw, I asked, DID YOU THROW FOOD AT THE FOOD FIGHT?" he bellowed.

"Yes," I said, scared, but determined to speak truth to power. "But someone threw it at me first."

"I didn't ask who threw it first, just answer me yes or no, did you or did you not throw food?"

"Yes," I said, looking down at my shoes, trying not to cry.

As my fifth-grade teacher, Mr. Kemp, used to say, while chewing on a toothpick, "Life's tough in the big city." The phrase was hilariously out of place in the small Illinois suburb where I grew up.

After my confession, F.J. Phillips bravely stepped forward.

"Mr. Nilsen," F.J. said. "She barely did anything."

"Oh," said Mr. Nilsen. "Okay."

Mr. Nilsen resumed his interrogation of the others and sent me home with a warning. His booming voice made me feel as if he had the power of life and death over me. I thought his sense of justice was arbitrary, and too loud.

Years later, I read his obituary. In 1987, when Mr. Nilsen was still principal, I was thirteen and already in middle school. At that time, a child named John Graziano became one of the first children in Illinois diagnosed with HIV. The pediatrician who diagnosed John refused to treat him. Another state over, in Indiana, a boy named Ryan White was shunned by his community and refused school entry when he was diagnosed with AIDS. In contrast, when John's parents first told Principal Nilsen about the diagnosis, Nilsen apparently said, firmly, "John stays in school." I listened to a piece on John by NPR's StoryCorps and learned that, at first, John's teachers would spray alcohol on John's desk for fear of contagion, and then Principal Nilsen said, "This is ridiculous. We're going to treat him no differently from any other child in the school."

John's family had hired a lawyer, anticipating possible blowback in the community, but it was a lawyer they never had to use. When the family left that first meeting with the principal—the principal who once intimidated me with his big scary voice—that principal sat down and did one thing, one of my teachers later told me. He cried.

When parents in the small community of Wilmette heard there was a child with HIV at Central Elementary School, some of them exploded. In 1987, there was a great deal of ignorance and panic. Some parents asked that John be taken out of school. Other parents demanded to know the child's identity so they could switch their children out of his classroom.

But Principal Nilsen refused to take John out of school, or disclose his identity to the other children, parents, or teachers who were uninvolved with his education. When a parent marched into their child's classroom and demanded to know which child in the class was HIV positive, Principal Nilsen said it was none of their business. Nilsen said, furthermore, that if anyone asked who in the classroom had AIDS, the children in the classroom would all raise their hands and say "We all have AIDS."

John died the day he would have turned ten. The memorial service was held at St. Francis church, and a handmade quilt covered John's small coffin. His friends sang "Happy Birthday" to him and ate birthday cake after the service. That spring, Principal Nilsen had a crab apple tree planted in John's honor outside the school. Students surrounded the tree and sang John's favorite song, which was "La Bamba." "Se necesita una poca de gracia . . . " *It takes a little grace, a little grace . . . To dance the Bamba.*

Principal Nilsen—who had been trained as a pastor—had been quietly heroic, and conjured grace, in our little town of Wilmette, Illinois. I learned after his death that sometimes, the people you fear, the people with loud scary voices, can also be the ones quietly doing enormous good.

Sunday school teachers and bullies

Normally Sister Kathy taught my weekly Sunday school at St. Francis Xavier Catholic Church, and we memorized lists of beatitudes and colored in pictures of Jesus. I don't remember getting any instruction on how to be kind. Which would have been helpful, as the class of Catholic girls were quite capable of petty meanness and treachery. They were, however, very skilled at staying in the lines when they colored in pictures of Jesus.

When I was twelve, Sister Kathy got sick and had to take a leave of absence. So, one day, Mr. Ivancovich rode in on his old bicycle to substitute teach our class. He was tall and skinny, with greasy black hair, round thick glasses, and he looked altogether like a giant crow, or how I imagined Ichabod Crane.

He focused less on Christ's loving message; instead, he seemed intent on scaring us to death with the gruesome biological details of Christ's crucifixion.

First, he said, the nails in Jesus's wrists would have ripped through the flesh. He detailed how Jesus suffocated up on that cross, how the weight of his body pushed down on his diaphragm, and how, to get more air, Jesus would have pushed his legs down, but there were nails pounded through the middle of his feet. Mr. Ivancovich led us through the minute-by-minute, excruciating scientific torture of a crucifixion. These intense details seemed to engage Mr. Ivancovich. Our eyes grew bigger and bigger with fear. We learned that human beings are capable of physically torturing others.

I can now extrapolate that, possibly in Mr. Ivancovich's mind, the lesson was that Christ suffered for our sins in a quite material way. But that lesson did not take root for me that day. I had questions. As the year progressed, leading up to my confirmation, I wanted to know why nuns couldn't speak to God whereas priests could. I wanted to know why, if the word *Catholic* meant "inclusive," we were supposed to look down on other religions and pick just one. I didn't understand why Jesus chose the *right* hand of the Father instead of the left. I didn't understand why, if God was compassionate, he would force people to go to hell if they were innocently born into the wrong religion. I had so many questions, and Mr. Ivancovich's style was not to answer questions. I would raise my hand, and he would ignore me; then again, he had very thick glasses, so he might not have seen me. The children were at Sunday school to memorize and receive. I memorized the Lord's Prayer, which I found comforting, but every time I tried to memorize the Nicene Creed I got stuck on certain phrases.

When I was thirteen, I decided not to get confirmed as a Catholic. When I announced my decision to leave the fold, the recriminations from the girls in my Sunday school class were immediate. One anonymous girl baked Star of David cookies and put them on my doorstep. Another girl got in my face at the playground and said, "What are you now, a Jew?"

And I wondered then, and now: How does regular old bullying lead to tribal bullying? Is tribal bullying an extension of the simple desire of one child to wield power over another? Did our Sunday school class need some other instructions on how to be kind, rather than lessons on the Romans' method of physical torture? I was no stranger to bullying on the playground, but religious mockery was new to me.

When I was growing up in the 1970s, kids mostly figured things out on their own; the bullied suffered in silence, trying to rise above shame. Bullies still pull hair, push kids downstairs, and all the rest of it—it's only that grown-ups and schools might be paying a little more attention these days. As Margaret Atwood wrote in *Cat's Eye*, "Little girls are cute and small only to adults. To one another they are not cute. They are life-sized."

What did my bully or bullies teach me? Back then, I had no psychological insight into the mind of a bully; I did not imagine how they might have been bullied at home. But as a child, I learned to accept that human nature is dark and full of unexpected poisons. And that organized religion can unfortunately be a place that shores up such poisons, rather than combatting them. I became wary. I avoided bullies. And found kind friends. I assumed that the ocean was large enough for minnows and sharks, and as I swam, I gave a wide berth to sharks.

I learned that if you are longing for companionship and a kind friend, you should seek out a kind friend and don't seek out a mean friend. Maybe this sounds overly simplistic, but the task is more complicated than it might first seem, and I believe it applies to one's love life too.

Over time, I became a playwright. What a wonderful way to control social situations. A playwright literally *puts words in other people's mouths*, and beautiful people will say them. You completely and silently control a social situation while people say your script. You can make human beings listen to each other, appear to fall in love, or mete out justice. Meanwhile, you can sit in a corner, watching, and contractually, no one can *not* say your words. What a magic power, a salve, a profound way to repair a social contract that might have been broken. And playwriting became, in its way for me, something of a religion.

Sisterhood is powerful

When I was twelve, my sister, Kate, four years older than me, cut my hair. I had long straight hair all the way down my back and needed a trim. Kate had read in a magazine that it was good to affix Scotch tape in a line to the hair, then cut above the line to keep the hair straight. I remember seeing Kate behind me in a full-length mirror, frowning, cutting above the tape, then cutting more, and more. The Scotch tape method wasn't quite working, so she kept cutting more hair, to get all the crooked off, until about six inches came off and I had to go to the barber to fix it.

I learned that when cutting a little sister's hair, don't use Scotch tape.

Kate and I had the same favorite childhood books. We were card-carrying members of the Betsy-Tacy Society. We knew many lines of that beloved series by heart. We both imagined ourselves as the heroine. I learned that sisters can both be the heroines of the books that we love.

Once, Kate and I were hiking up a mountain in Ireland and heard a scream. A little redheaded girl, a stranger, had fallen down a cliff, and her elderly great-aunts were looking down the cliff in horror. I screamed and looked away, but my sister ran toward danger and pulled that girl up from a mountainous crevice.

When a doctor arrived, it was clear that the girl's leg was broken, and she wailed plaintively, "I'm going to miss Saint Paddy's Day!"

I looked at my sister; we both knew that girl could have died. I learned then and there that my sister runs toward physical danger, and I look away. Doctors learn to run toward danger when a code is run in the emergency room. My sister became a doctor.

There are different kinds of strength, and by one measure my sister is much, much stronger than me, always has been, always will be. My strength is quieter and not really in my body. When we were little, my sister and I measured our strength against each other. It was never a fair fight—she was older and stronger, and I'd be on the floor pinned down, and she'd let her spit dangle in my face before deciding to suck it back up at the last minute. Siblings teach each other to fight the way that dogs learn to fight, by sparring.

It was okay if my sister kicked me in that special place on my leg that made me topple over, but it was not okay if my bully did that—if anyone outside my family hurt me, my sister would exact vengeance. When sisters grow up, maybe they stop measuring their strength against one another. I watch my own daughters measure their strength against each other. I don't like it, but I know it is what sisters do.

Other things my sister taught me:

- How to funny phone call your bully.
- Most things are funny. Like, literally, almost everything. If you look at them askance.
- How to go on a roller coaster.
- How to broil a hot dog in a toaster oven, char it, slice it down the middle, and melt cheddar cheese on top.
- How to shoot a basketball.
- Most fun does not require planning.
- Happiness can be measured by how many of your friends stop by your house unexpectedly.
- People feel things deeply even when they don't say so.
- And: the childhood kingdom you shared with your sister will never go away as long as you are both alive to remember it together.

When middle C is not the middle

"This is middle C." That is the first thing I remember learning from my piano teacher, Mrs. Rubenstein. Music teachers are often the only teachers young people have from childhood through adolescence; as a result, they know children in a way that none of their other teachers can.

I was an indifferent pianist, but I loved music. And I loved my piano lessons. They were every Monday night. I listened to my sister play first, then I got to play. Mrs. Rubenstein was tiny and full of energy, like a sparrow; unlike a bird, she seemed to subsist entirely on Diet Coke. She wore round glasses that magnified her already large brown eyes, and her tiny face was all eyes and cheekbones. She liked to make up puns about music and give out candy. She'd start the year by giving out cards containing a stick of gum; the card read "Good job *sticking* to piano." She taught us to play music Suzuki style, mostly by ear, eventually teaching us to read music, which was so much harder for me than reading books.

Sometimes Mrs. Rubenstein would play chords with her left hand on the piano, and I would improvise melodies on the right. Or we would play a duet together. I worked hard at my Bach minuets. I composed little tragical songs. My sister composed cheerful songs. The passage of time felt slow and beautiful while I waited for my sister's lesson to be over, listening to her play. I would read, or roll around on the floor, or sit on my mother's lap, feeling safe and held. I dream of my piano lessons not infrequently.

My sister and I never practiced much at home. The serious and gifted Lieberman sisters had a lesson right before us, and sometimes we heard the tail end of their lesson from the hall; the "Moonlight Sonata" floated out to us in the hallway, while we were still on Suzuki book one. I have no doubt the Lieberman sisters had more natural talent than we had and also practiced a great deal. But my sister and I shared the delusion that, though the Lieberman sisters were definitely better than us at piano, maybe Mrs. Rubenstein liked us more because we were amusing.

It was evident from the start that I was never going to become a concert pianist; what, then, was the value of the particular relationship I had with my music teacher? For one thing, she taught me to love and read music. When I found myself at the age of forty-eight in a rehearsal room at the Metropolitan Opera, having written a libretto for composer Matthew Aucoin, I could sit at my table, confidently read the score, and know where to turn the pages. I could plunk out the melody on the piano at home. And, more important, I could talk to the composer about music and tone.

But even if my writing life had never taken a turn toward collaborating with musicians, this long friendship with my piano teacher—with a grown-up who cared deeply for me and my sister—helped us in a way that no economist could parse in terms of value:

She thought we were worth teaching.

She taught us how to practice.

She taught us how to sit up straight.

How to show up every week.

How much dull repetition it takes to make something beautiful.

And perhaps most important—she taught us how to make a mistake in the music and keep playing, keep moving forward.

Learning how to make a mistake and go forward is a skill kids need so desperately, no matter the art form. For kids who are perfectionists, having a stable adult figure holding space for imperfection with grounded love is of great consequence. Maybe I even learned lessons about imperfection *better* from Mrs. Rubenstein because I was not a gifted pianist. I learned that I could be mediocre at something and still love it deeply.

Mrs. Rubenstein had two sons, and she spoke about them in our regular chitchat between lessons. One of her sons struck up a friendship with my sister, even taking her to his high school prom, one town away. He eventually became a weatherman in California. Mrs. Rubenstein's other son died tragically early.

I didn't see Mrs. Rubenstein very much after she lost her son. We were too old for piano lessons, and we'd gone off to college. I saw her briefly at my father's funeral. I observed that she seemed to have gotten even tinier, her eyes bigger, her face smaller. But she survived. And moved forward. And she kept teaching music to young children.

"This is middle C."

Just the thought of that phrase describes a world that is certain, understandable, capable of being mastered. Life does not always comport with the beautiful certitudes of music, or the stable placement of the middle.

Middle C does not move. But the middle of a life is never certain; we never know where the middle is until life ends. We long for there to be plenty of room below middle C, and plenty of room above. But sometimes a song stops short and is no less beautiful for its brevity.

The perfect bookstore

My childhood bookstore was, to me, perfect. Maybe it could have existed only when I was a child, because perfection requires the filter of memory. It was called, in its plainspoken way, the Wilmette Bookstore, and I could walk there. Its first perfection: *proximity*.

The second perfection: *size*. My childhood bookstore was small, and cozy. Probably about the size of a modest studio apartment in Brooklyn. It had piles and piles of books, almost falling over, sections too high for me to reach, and ladders. It did not have useless, arcane, and specialized sections—books you don't want to read. Nor did it sell toys or stuffed animals. It sold just one thing: books. It didn't even sell day planners or fancy pens. The book itself was object enough for imagination; the store did not attempt to engage the senses in any other way but the promise of language and story.

In my small childhood bookstore, it felt like the limitations of the walls were almost akin to the limitations of a body—and one could read everything inside, until the next shipment of books came. There was no café, no large children's section with fuzzy chairs. In fact, the bookstore was so small, there was no place to read except standing up.

Some bookstores have now become so big, I get confused wandering around. So many stuffed animals leering at me! So many books—I feel guilty I haven't read them all! And what is it about franchises that feels unromantic? Is it that they all smell vaguely the same and so could be anywhere? Is it the uniforms? The lack of dust?

The Wilmette Bookstore was owned by two older women. In retrospect, they seemed like a couple, but one was married to the town mayor. One was tall and lean with soft shoulder-length white hair and round glasses that magnified her sea-green eyes—Joan. She moved slowly, her long arms reaching up high to get the books I couldn't reach. The other owner was short and scrappy with a gravelly voice (a smoker?)—Barbara. She moved fast. Both ladies recognized me when I came in.

The third perfection: *being known.*

When I was a child at the Wilmette Bookstore, Barbara and Joan would say, "What do I have that Sarah would want to read next?" They would reach up high or get on a ladder and pull down an unknown book for me. How does one know what to read when one hasn't read it yet? It is a conundrum for readers and learners going all the way back to Plato, who identified the paradox of learning—how can we know what we do not yet know? When I was a child, Barbara and Joan knew for me.

One time I saved up enough of my own money for a book that had to be ordered—the next book in my beloved Betsy-Tacy series. When I got to the store, Barbara winked and said they'd sold it already. Then she laughed and gave it to me.

The fourth perfection: *browsing.* I love the simple ritual of browsing while standing up—looking at and being with a book rather than possessing it. Because you can't really possess books you love. They possess you.

When I was eighteen, I had a summer job at a local bookstore called the Book Stall. I was a terrible employee. The poetry section was behind a short wall; I pretended to restock while I was secretly bending over and reading poems.

I remember the first time I could browse again in a bookstore after the pandemic—one full year of no browsing in person. It was the Savoy bookstore in Westerly, Rhode Island—a very beautiful bookstore—and I wept in the children's section for sheer relief at being among physical books again. I inhaled the smell of books and relished being in proximity to the small number of booklovers around me, wearing masks.

The Wilmette Bookstore closed around the time I went off to college. Before Amazon existed, and before you could read books on cell phones. It closed in the era of paper. New bookstores have entered my heart, where I live or where I wander. But this childhood memory remains indelible—a bookstore-as-hideout, one where I was known and respected as a small reader. When Joan and Barbara recommended books to young readers, their eyes lit up, and I don't think that illumination was about an imminent sale. Their eyes lit up as if, when they handed me a book, they were transmitting to me a love for the written word. I walked out of their shop with a new world in my small hands.

Joyce Piven, and how to listen

I was a shy child, often sick, for weeks at a time. I'd stay home from school, losing myself in books. But I loved going to the theater. My mother was an actress, and I loved going to rehearsals with her. She encouraged me and my sister to act in plays, and we did, although I would get terribly nervous before going onstage, my heart pounding. My voice was small and did not carry far.

When I was twelve, my mother signed me up for after-school acting lessons at the Piven Theatre Workshop in Evanston, Illinois, founded by the famed Joyce and Byrne Piven, who both trained generations of Chicago actors. The first time I met Joyce Piven, she was visiting my class, taught by her daughter Shira Piven (who is now an acclaimed director in her own right). Joyce favored dark tunics and black pants and heavy silver belts. She had a short pixie cut and looked as though she could step into an avant-garde production of Macbeth at a moment's notice. She had a deep throaty voice, and incredibly expressive brown eyes. She was intimidating, and I immediately craved her approval. She wanted to teach us the art of transformation. Nothing less satisfied her.

Once, demonstrating how to act in a fairy tale, she turned herself into an ancient witch in front of our eyes. That was the first time I witnessed how third-person narration could enact physical transformation in the theater. I was gobsmacked. Joyce disappeared into the role of a crone with nothing but her body and a few improvised phrases.

When I was fourteen, I took her scene-study class. My acting partner, a sweet fellow my age, and I rehearsed our little romantic scene before presenting it. The stage directions called for a kiss, but we ignored it while rehearsing. Then, when we did our scene for the class, he kissed me, and I must have jumped. Joyce said to him in her husky voice, "Oh no, you have to plan those things in advance with your scene partner . . ." It was, in fact, my first kiss, and Joyce had witnessed it.

Joyce would go on to witness or instigate so many of my firsts, both theatrical and personal. When I started writing poetry and plays, Joyce was an early champion. It was clear (to me, abundantly) that I was no actor. That didn't matter to Joyce. She cultivated talent where she saw it—acting, writing, or simply being a person. She commissioned my first professional play, and then directed it. We watched rehearsals together when actors were brilliant and inventive; we also watched when actors were unable to go on.

I remember one actress who flung herself on the ground and groaned, "I'm in the tunnel!"

Joyce looked at her and said, "Then get up!"

Later she told me and our dear collaborator Polly Noonan: "Every production is a battlefield. Some people go down. Some people are heroes. Others leave the field of battle altogether."

Joyce always modeled and understood the importance of family alongside the difficult work of being an artist. I saw her for lunch the day I got engaged to my husband. "Ah!" she said with a note of triumph. "You're going to marry *a doctor!*" When Joyce's husband, Byrne Piven, died, she was bereft. She said it was her job to mourn him for the rest of her life, and to carry on his legacy. She said that, without him, every day was a stone, and that if she put one stone on the ground in front of another stone, and then another, eventually there would be a path for her to walk forward. She produced an absurdist play of mine called *Melancholy Play* (about a woman who is so sad she turns into an almond) soon thereafter, and I heard Joyce laughing, watching my play, sitting behind me. I was glad to be able to make her laugh in the midst of grief. I've always thought one of the most important functions of theater is to comfort the grieving.

I visited Joyce in the hospital when she was in her eighties. She'd had a terrifying mystery infection that went awry, causing cycling fevers and hallucinations. She called herself Adrienne (her middle name) and spoke French. She asked me and our friend Polly to read Shakespeare aloud to her. As we read, she would continue to coach Polly on her acting, even while in the hospital.

"Stop, Polly," she'd say. "Read it again, that line should be a demonstration of amazement."

Then I painted her fingernails a nice dark red. I told Joyce before I left the hospital that I'd missed her, and she said, "I've missed you and missed you and finally I thought if I miss you, then you must miss me."

"I do," I said.

In a strange turn of affairs, my doctor sister was called in to direct Joyce's care, because Chicago is a small world. My sister eventually got Joyce stable, figuring out that it was a urinary tract infection causing the hallucinations and prescribing her the right medicines so that she could leave the hospital.

The last time I saw Joyce, she was ninety-three years old, and living in Los Angeles. She'd had several falls, and the doctor told her no more walking, because her next fall could be her last. So she was seated on her couch, wearing her usual fashionable black tunic, with a big silver belt, her face made-up. Books surrounded her.

I asked her how she was. She said, in her throaty, passionate, unhurried, and unmistakable cadence, "I'm not thriving, but I'm alive, and I'm going to stay here on this earth until they kick me out. I'm stubborn, and I'm faithful, and I have good references."

And she shook her fist at the sky.

We talked of books, and of her childhood. She'd never spoken to me of her childhood before, and now for some reason, her childhood, on the South Side of Chicago, seemed very present to her. She spoke of the endless work her mother did at a deli to support the family. And how her father, a charismatic ne'er-do-well, taught her how to tell a good story, which she credits with getting her out of relative poverty.

When it was time for me to leave, Joyce said she'd walk me to the door.

I said, "No need to walk me to the door. The nurse said no walking, because you can't have another fall, right?"

"I'll *walk you to the door*," she said. "Let me show you what I can do. I've been practicing."

Joyce asked her aide for her walker.

The aide said, "Joyce, you know you're not supposed to be walking…"

Joyce simply gestured to her walker, like a queen. Her aide sighed and brought her the walker. I got on one side of Joyce, and her aide got on the other side, and Joyce grabbed her walker, standing up. She walked with surprising speed to the door with us on either side, just in case. At the door, I told her how much I loved her, how much she'd taught me.

"That," she whispered, "is the gift."

Then she sat back down in her wheelchair, and I walked into the bright sunlight.

A year later, Joyce would be in the hospital with pneumonia. She couldn't speak, but her daughter Shira held up the phone to her ear so I could speak to her. I wanted to read a fragment of *The Tempest* to her, the one she used to have us repeat in class, exploring and heightening the words:

Full fathom five thy father lies;
Of his bones are coral made;
Those are pearls that were his eyes:
Nothing of him that doth fade,
But doth suffer a sea-change
Into something rich and strange.

I wanted to remind Joyce that she'd been transforming all her life, so this latest transformation was nothing to fear. Knowing that she was listening, even though she couldn't speak, I trusted that she heard every word. After all, Joyce had always taught us the art of listening. She would say, "Nothing is more beautiful on stage than someone really listening. Not *pretending* to listen. But really listening. Not thinking of what they are about to say next. Not anticipating. Not performing the act of listening. But *listening*." She trained thousands of people how to listen with empathy and presence; how to listen to the spaces between the words.

So when I read Shakespeare on the phone to her, I knew with every fiber of my being that she was listening, even though she could not speak. When I was a shy child, Joyce taught me how to play without self-consciousness; when I was a teenager, she taught me how language can transform space; when I was a young woman, and had lost my father, she taught me how grief can transform into art; and when I was a grown artist, she taught me how to endure. I can't really imagine not having more conversations with her, so I think I'll just go on having them. Somewhere, not out of reach, is her deep, wide listening: her love.

Rilke and the romance of solitude

Oh, I was such a lonely eighteen-year-old.

I wandered around my college campus in Providence, Rhode Island, clutching a copy of Rainer Maria Rilke's *Letters to a Young Poet* to my bosom, dog-earing it, underlining, rereading. "Be patient toward all that is unsolved in your heart," Rilke told me, "and try to love the questions themselves." I was full of longing, besotted with the beauty of solitude, deeply inside all my poetic dreams, and I could not find a container for these invisible yearnings. At night, I couldn't sleep. I lay awake, in a place so different from my Midwestern home, my mind sifting through fragments of the books I'd read all day—philosophy, novels, poetry, feminism . . .

Meanwhile, in Chicago, my father was dying of cancer. I was not walking or driving distance away; I was a plane ride away. I was deeply homesick, and I had to go into the air to get back to my roots. My mother procured an application to the University of Chicago, encouraging me to transfer, but my father was determined I should stay at Brown University and not let his condition affect my education. Did he somehow divine I'd meet my husband there? Or that I'd meet a playwriting teacher who would alter the course of my life?

At any rate, I poured myself into my studies, pursued friendships with highly intelligent beings who had little notion of my emotional state, and I slept very little. I had a close circle of friends in the Midwest, many of them, weirdly, also named Sarah. (Maybe not so weird; it was one of the most popular baby names in the 1970s.) None of my friends came east for school. At Brown University, the social hierarchies mystified me; everyone seemed to have gone to the same New York City private school and seemed to know one another already. They also seemed to have already taken ancient Greek, and classes like Satire and Sentiment in the Nineteenth-Century Novel; whereas at my very good public school I had taken English or History. The people who lived on my dorm floor were highly developed ironists, and they smoked a *lot* of pot. A good number had famous parents, many were deeply depressed, and sometimes I'd find one curled in the fetal position in the hallway on the floor after a rave. I could have used an excellent therapist, but when I went to health services, hoping to get some sleeping aids, the therapist threw some Elizabeth Kübler Ross at me about the five stages of grief, which offended me because my father wasn't dead yet. Then she accused me of being aloof, so I never returned. (Which, looking back, is an aloof thing to do.)

Instead, I chose Rilke for my own private soul teacher. Going through a heartbreak? Have a first love who was possessive? Pull out Rilke, who would whisper to me across the ages: "I hold this to be the highest task of a bond between two people: that each should stand guard over the solitude of the other." Desperate to write poetry? Walk among the spring blossoms, carrying Rilke. "Look deep into your heart where it spreads its roots . . . and ask yourself, must I write?" Wandering the cold, damp, winter streets of Providence unable to sleep at five in the morning with no kith or kin to hold you? Rilke whispered to me: "But your solitude will be a hold and home for you, even amid very unfamiliar circumstances, and from it you will find all your paths."

For years, the reading public only had Rilke's letters *to* but not *from* the young poet; that part of the dialogue was lost to history until Franz's (the young poet's) letters were found and published this past year along with Rilke's. At eighteen, I had been reading a one-sided conversation, with access to none of the questions from the young wisdom-seeking Franz. Was Franz boring? I wondered. Or just humble, and embarrassed of his youthful questions? Perhaps the fact that the conversation was one-sided in print made it easier to project my own life onto the letters; it felt as if *I* were writing my questions to Rilke, and he was writing back to me, through the centuries.

This year, I bought the updated *Letters to a Young Poet* with Franz's newly published letters to Rilke, thinking it would be a revelation to read the two of them in dialogue. But if I thought I'd find the secret to teaching, or life, in Franz's letters, I was disappointed. In his letters, Franz was sweet, flattering. He was serving in the military and sick of its banal hierarchies; he asked Rilke to read his rather insipid poetry and circulate it; Rilke demurred. Franz was also ambitious to write plays. ("I am planning to write a play. The hero will be an officer . . . his little struggles and great disappointments . . . will be based on mine.") Franz was at times suicidal; no wonder Rilke wrote him with such a burning spiritual force, as if to save his young friend's life. Maybe he did save young Franz's life. Franz was tortured by love. Franz fell hard for a woman trained as an opera singer in Vienna, and she was forced into marrying a man in Constantinople, but she would at times run back to Franz, before disappearing into the Balkans. Franz seemed to deeply misconstrue love, writing that he loved a young woman so much that he wanted to kill her. No wonder Rilke felt the need to lay down his own philosophy of love, which insisted upon boundaries.

If I learned anything from Franz's newly published letters, it was that Rilke was beyond generous and patient. And that Franz was duly grateful, expressing his gratitude fulsomely. "Honored sir," he wrote, "I truly don't know how I can thank you. When I think that all these unsayable, marvelous, beautiful things you've entrusted to me are meant for me alone—that you find me worthy of sharing in these riches, meant only for the few, the solitary—I feel very proud."

How lucky for us that Rilke's words, while they were addressed to Franz, were not meant for Franz alone but for future generations. Franz had the foresight to share Rilke's letters with the world, publishing them three years after Rilke's death, omitting his own letters, and writing in his introduction, "Where a great, unique man speaks, lesser men can only fall silent."

And yet it is in the *dialogue* with Franz that Rilke's teaching began. My copy of *Letters to a Young Poet*, dog-eared and wept through, got me through some of my loneliest moments. It's possible that Rilke taught me to like my solitude a little too much. In time, I learned that I would be better served by being in dialogue with the living, breathing, responsive teachers who were all around me.

My father and words as nourishment

Every Saturday, when I was a child, my father would take me to breakfast at Walker Brothers Pancake House, a place out of time in the suburbs of Chicago, full of stained glass and massive Dutch pancakes. My father taught me a new word every week. The ritual was holy to me. He would tell me the etymology, along with the word, so I could remember it.

Peripatetic. Wandering around speaking in weighty matters, from the Greek.

Ostracize, from the Greek, from those white pieces of pottery people used to vote out offending community members. (*Ostracize* was particularly useful to me, at certain points in my elementary school life.)

Defunct. Dead, in a very abrupt way. The word reminded me of my father's favorite E. E. Cumming's poem, "Buffalo Bill's Defunct."

Unlike Buffalo Bill, who died all at once, in cowboy boots, my father died slowly, over the course of two hard-fought years, when he was fifty-three, of cancer. But death is always, at the very last moment, abrupt.

My father was diagnosed with cancer when I was eighteen, a month after I started college. A quick-witted, healthy, active, broad-shouldered man, he was having some back pain. Being no stranger to back pain, he ignored it for a while, until he couldn't walk. He had an MRI; his body was riddled with cancer. It was in the bones, organs, and lymph nodes.

I, meanwhile, was deep in the self-absorption of college life and knew nothing of his MRI. I was homesick and couldn't sleep. I wandered the streets of Providence at four in the morning after being up all night with insomnia, hoping the Dunkin' Donuts would finally open. I would call home and complain about my sleeplessness. One weekend in October, my whole family arrived in Providence to visit me.

Wow, they even brought my sister, I thought, *they must be really concerned about me.*

I noticed that my dad was walking with a cane. Back pain, he said.

I took them on a tour of campus, showed them the women's center where I was volunteering.

"This looks like a nice, quiet place," my mother said. "Let's sit down and talk."

They led me to a couch in the library, shut the door. My dad nodded at my mom. And she told me that he had a very serious cancer. My father's chin trembled, but he did not cry.

That weekend, we drove around the shores of Rhode Island, looked at the sea and the changing leaves. My parents took me and a couple of new friends out for Chinese food. After dinner, we read all our fortunes from our fortune cookies. My father opened his. It was blank. Everyone looked away. I almost couldn't bear to say goodbye to my family that weekend.

I came home from college at every opportunity. A friend whose father traveled constantly donated frequent-flier miles to us, and I used them to fly home to Chicago as much as I could. One day, at home on a break, I saw my father walking to the bathroom, and his pants fell down around his ankles; he had lost so much weight, and he couldn't pull his pants up by himself. My mother came running. I knew this was one of the many things he did not want me to see—and why he wanted me back at college, pretending things were normal.

My father had an ability to make jokes that would put other people at ease while he was suffering. He escaped his physical suffering by putting the focus on us, or a nurse, or a friend. He had recently left the Catholics of his childhood and joined the Congregational church. He was keen not to cancel a trip he'd signed up for with the Congregational church to help build houses for the unhoused.

That spring, my whole family went to South Carolina to build a house. It's hard for me to imagine now the pain he must have felt in his bones while he swung a hammer on that trip; in the photos, he looks happy, although he'd lost most of his hair. My father never asked the doctors how much time he had. He refused prognostications. I learned, years later, from my mother that they thought he had, at most, six months from the time of diagnosis. He lived more than two years.

When he finally landed in the hospital for the last time, experimental radiation had lowered his white blood count significantly, and his lungs were full of cancer. I read poetry to him. The whole extended family gathered around. He told us to play "When the Saints Go Marching In" at his funeral. And he died while a full moon rose outside the window.

I learned in those two years what a quiet hero looks like. My father never met my husband or my children. I dreamed once that he met my husband, Tony, and my father told me in the dream that it was a good idea to marry him. My father loved having smart daughters and one of his mantras was "marry your intellectual equal."

In my early twenties, desperate to have more conversations with my father, I wrote a play called *Eurydice*. I imagined the sort of letter my father might write on my wedding day. I wrote:

If I were to give a speech at your wedding, I would start with one or two funny jokes and then I might offer some words of advice. I would say:

Cultivate the arts of dancing and small talk.

Everything in moderation.

Court the companionship and respect of dogs.

Grilling a fish or toasting bread without burning requires singleness of purpose, vigilance, and steadfast watching.

Keep quiet about politics, but vote for the right man. Or woman.

Take care to change the light bulbs.

Continue to give yourself to others because that's the ultimate satisfaction in life—to love, accept, honor, and help others.

The last two lines of that soliloquy I borrowed from a letter my father wrote me while I was at college. He warned me about the dangers of solipsism, which he knew could be found in the writing life. He knew I wanted to be a writer, even though he didn't know I became one. In the last letter my father wrote me before he died, he started with E. E. Cummings and Joe Gould:

Joseph Ferdinand Gould, self-styled "Last of the Bohemians" slept on park benches, in hallways, and subways, and was occasionally picked up for vagrancy. Joe also wrote poetry. His verse was terse, viz—

"In winter I'm a Buddhist,

"And in summer I'm a nudist."

Last week you and I were talking about one of the trite themes identified by joe gould—love. Cummings had some nice words to say on this subject. Years later, when a publisher decided to issue a selection of George Herriman's panels, cummings was asked to write the introduction. He wrote it with love, and love is his theme. "A lot of people 'love' because, and a lot of people 'love' although, and a few individuals love. Love is something illimitable and a lot of people spend their limited lives trying to prevent anything illimitable from happening to them."

I'm humble that you have provided illimitable love to me. I hope you realize that my love for you is also illimitable. Whatever happens in the crazy twisting and turnings of my current situation, I know I can fall back on the love between us as one of the rocks in my life. Continue to grow and mature into womanhood. You have much to contribute to the world—I am only grateful that I've been one of the beneficiaries. You will always be in my thoughts this semester, and I look forward to spending the summer (maybe as Buddhists) with you pondering (love thou art frail) why some love can be illimitable.

Cummings used the word *illimitable*. He might also have used the word *unconditional*. My father loved his children without conditions. How did he do this? Did he simply luck into this capacity, some trifecta of temperament, upbringing, and the stars? Can you teach the capacity for unconditional love, and can you imitate it by example? Was it still inside me after he died? I think so.

For a long time, I carried my father's letter with me wherever I moved, putting it in my desk for good luck. As a child, he gave me words along with food, and so I associated words with nourishment, and love. After he died, I took a scrap of his handwriting and put it in my wallet to keep me company. I would look at his handwriting if I was on a plane and afraid to die; I thought if I died, I'd go straight to the letters, the source, the relation. I tried to grow up, tried to know on a cellular level that I'd absorbed the words, absorbed the love. Time passed, and eventually, I no longer needed his handwriting to fly.

Paula Vogel

I met the playwright Paula Vogel at Brown University in a playwriting class when I was twenty. I'd just taken a leave of absence after my father's death. When I came back to school, I found it hard to read, and to write. I was in mourning, distracted. I kept reading the same page over and over again, staring at the page. And I was surrounded by twenty-year-olds drunk on booze or young love.

Paula suggested we meet in person mid-semester to talk about my unwritten play at Café Zog on Wickenden Street. She bought me a cookie. I was nervous to take the cookie; should I let a teacher pay for my nourishment when she already was giving me so many other kinds of nourishment? It seemed like too much to ask for. But I took the cookie. Maybe she could see that I was sad; she could see pretty much everything. When I told her that I was having trouble writing about the things that mattered most to me because of my father's death, she gazed at me intently.

She told me, "If someone asked me to write a play about my brother Carl, who died of AIDS, I would never have gotten out of bed. Instead, I wrote about a kindergarten teacher with a mystery illness taking a trip through Europe with her brother, which became my play *Baltimore Waltz*. And I was able to write about Carl."

I had recently seen *The Baltimore Waltz* in a black box theater at the university. The play is dedicated to Paula's brother, and it's a cathartic, surreal, absurdist, highly personal play. I hadn't read it beforehand, and at the end, when the ghost of Carl waltzes with his sister, I was bowled over with grief. I went to the play with my best friend, Kirsten, who had lost her father to AIDS, and we clung to each other and wept long after the play was over.

Paula explained to me, while I ate my cookie at Café Zog, that sometimes you have to look at grief sideways or upside down, just as you shouldn't look directly at the sun, and assign yourself formal tricks to write about the most difficult subjects.

Then she looked at me with that uncanny penetrating gaze of hers and said, "I want you to write a play in which a dog is the protagonist."

"Okay," I said. And I did. It was the first thing I was able to write after my father died. The play was called *Dog Play* and viewed my father's illness and death through the eyes of the family dog. The dog spoke this soliloquy:

DOG: He's dying. They don't have to tell me, I know. I can see it in the way the walls look now that they've gone. And they didn't even take me with to say goodbye. I'm not allowed in the hospitals. Germs. The house is quiet—his cane is watching me from the corner. Last night, when the ambulances came, I didn't even bark. I knew. I didn't bite the big men who came in—dwarfing the small rooms in their boots—their virility making the smell of death in the house seem absurd—impossible. They lifted him into a chair—they carried him down the stairs on a throne, and he was as dignified as a king, in spite of the baby elephant tubing on his mouth and the baby duck hair on his head. I tried to say goodbye to him—but mostly I tried not to get in the way.

Paula taught me how to liberate my plays from the usual narrative arc with her critique of Aristotle's theatrical structure. But what strikes me most when I remember Paula's teaching is her *presence* as much as the content of her teachings. In this country, we are obsessed with content and curriculum, all the while devaluing presence and proximity, which are two teaching values hard to describe or quantify (or, indeed, teach).

My senior year, I asked Paula to be my thesis adviser. I wanted to write a scholarly thesis on representations of the actress in the Victorian novel.

Paula said, "No, I cannot advise that thesis."

I was devastated for a moment, until she said quickly, "It's not my area of expertise. But if you write a play, I will advise your thesis."

I felt a strangled joy in my chest. I had an idea for a play, which would become my first full-length play, *Passion Play*. Could I choose joy? Could I write a *play*? It seemed too decadent, too fun. I wrote the play, meeting with Paula every week at Café Zog so she could read ten pages at a time. The play poured out of me. It seemed easier to write a full-length play than I thought it should be.

Knowing that I began my writing life as a rather retiring poet, Paula treated me with much tenderness and guile, sneaking my play into a new plays festival. This is one of Paula's chosen teaching methods, which she fully admits. She attempts to make students addicted to the magic of the dust backstage. I already had a predisposition to loving theater's back-stage dust because of my actress mother, and I inhaled some more during *Passion Play* rehearsals.

My mother flew into town from Chicago to Providence to see the play. On opening night, my mother and I were driving down the hill toward Trinity Repertory Company when we were blindsided, hit by a car going very fast on Hope Street. (The names in Providence make for good allegory.) I wasn't wearing a seat belt in the back seat, and I hit my head and blacked out. Before I blacked out, I remember thinking: *This is how death comes, quickly.*

I woke up, and my mother thought maybe we should go to the hospital for an MRI, and I said, "Are you kidding? Let's go to my play, we're almost late." So we went to my play, and I remember an out-of-body sense of rapture when I saw my play in three dimensions, with actors acting and people watching and, finally, the audience all standing as if one body and applauding. I knew then that I would spend my life doing this and not look back.

When I got an MRI the following day, it was normal. It did not register the change of vocation.

Three years later, when I was in graduate school for playwriting, Paula took me and two other writing students to her beautiful home in Cape Cod. She had us look out at the wide expanse of ocean and told us to say to ourselves, "This is what playwriting can buy." Paula's play *How I Learned to Drive* was the Pulitzer Prize–winning juggernaut that bought the house with the beautiful view. The play begins, "Sometimes to tell a secret, you first have to teach a lesson." The play is an impressionistic, beautiful, heartbreaking tale of a young woman whose uncle assaults her while he teaches her how to drive. I had seen the first reading of this play at the Vineyard Theatre in New York City, starring Cherry Jones, when I was twenty-one years old. I had seen Paula's grief at the first out-loud reading of the play; I sat in the row behind her and watched as her partner, Anne, put an arm around her shoulders to steady her.

This past summer, our kids now grown, we made our ritual end-of-the-summer visit to Cape Cod to see Paula and her wife, Anne, to swim in ponds, gather oysters, and play Scrabble. And Paula helped teach my older daughter, Anna, how to drive.

I've always known how much Paula loves driving, despite the complicated valences it has in that highly personal play. In real life, Paula takes the wheel of a car and evinces control, freedom, and power over the road. I knew there was no better driving teacher for my daughter. Paula taught Anna how to adjust the mirrors. How to choose good music for driving. How to lead with confidence. And how to approach an intersection. Paula said to Anna, "Always make yourself visible, so other drivers can see you coming."

When I took Anna out to practice driving later, she inched right up to an intersection, saying, "Paula taught me: *At a crossroads, make yourself visible, so people can see you coming.*" I thought, *My God, what an important lesson for Anna to get from this woman who taught me so much of what I know.* And I think of the twenty-year-old me with my Midwestern reticence, who walked into Paula's classroom, where she taught me much the same thing. *"Make yourself visible."*

The question of whether playwriting is teachable begets other questions, like: Is devotion teachable? Is listening teachable? Is a love of art and a willingness to give your life over to art teachable? I believe that these things are teachable mostly by example, and in great silences. There is the wondrous noise of the classroom, the content, the liveliness of the teachings themselves, the exchange of knowledge, and then there is the great silence of relation. Of seeing how great people live. How they eat, how they love, how they drive. When I reflect on all the things Paula taught me—among them bravery, stick-to-itiveness, how to write a play in forty-eight hours, how to write stage directions that are both impossible to stage and possible to stage—the greatest of these is love. Love for the art form, love for fellow writers, and love for the world.

Ancient Tragedy and Its Influence

The class Ancient Tragedy and Its Influence was early in the morning (challenging for an insomniac like me in college back then), but I was almost always wide awake because the professor was so entertaining. The balding, bearded, bespectacled professor, David Konstan, seemed to know as much about Mel Brooks as he did about Euripides, which was a great deal. Little did I know my future husband was also taking the course. We were in different sections and never met that year, but both of us were contemplating the social and political ramifications of Racine versus Sophocles at 9:00 a.m. on any given Thursday.

I remember the readings from that semester vividly; reading Arthur Miller's essay on tragedy and the modern man, and Anouilh's *Antigone* may have mightily influenced my playwriting. But what I remember even more than the readings was the sheer *presence* of David. He had his advisees over to his house at the end of the semester, where he made baba ghanoush by roasting eggplants *in his fireplace*. They crackled and smoked. This was a revelation. I had never eaten fresh baba ghanoush before, nor had I ever seen an eggplant in a fireplace. The smoky delicious taste was new and nourishing, as was the conversation.

I took a class with Professor Konstan the following year, this time a small seminar on the nature of friendship in the ancient and modern world. We contrasted Aristotelian friendship with Platonic friendship. We had a look at Emerson's thoughts on the matter, Seneca's too; and we thought about friendship in the *Aeneid*. I wrote a twenty-page dialogue about the nature of friendship with my best friend at the time, a young passionate French intellectual named Justine.

After my father died, David Konstan wrote to me, a real-life letter in a real envelope, and we started a correspondence that continued when I took a semester off from college to mourn. I was staying with my mother and sister in the suburbs of Chicago and teaching special education by day. By afternoon, everything seemed dark. When David was invited to the University of Chicago to give a lecture that fall, he invited me for coffee, and we took a bracing walk by Lake Michigan on the South Side. I tried to put a brave Midwestern face on my sadness, but David saw through my attempt at stoicism. As a classicist, he knew all about the Stoics, and my raw grief was nowhere near Seneca's mettle. The cold spray whipped up from the jetty. And David talked to me about life and death. He wasn't obliged, as a professor, to give me fatherly advice by a lake in my time of grief, but he took the time.

I might never have had the courage to go back to Providence the following semester if I hadn't known a teacher in the way that I knew David; someone who opened his home to his students; someone who thought the ancients had something compelling to tell us about how to live life now, how to face grief now. On a stone building on campus, these words are etched: "Speak to the past and it shall teach thee."

Three years ago, David came to my opera version of *Eurydice* (a play about the loss of my father, in a classical container) at the Metropolitan Opera. David walked down the red velvet aisle, and we peered into the orchestra pit together at intermission. *Eurydice* probably owed a huge debt to my learning about ancient tragedy from David. After the opera, we drank wine across the street, he told me about his new book about the history of forgiveness, and he regaled me with stories about teaching comedy, ancient and modern, at NYU. Here was a man who had been a father figure to me when I sorely needed one. He met my father once, when my dad visited me at college, and David told my father that he would act in loco parentis while I was at school, making a joke about *loco* meaning "crazy" in addition to meaning "in place of."

David taught me that the ancient texts were vehicles that writers used over and over again through history, that they spoke to every era differently, but also that they were accessible and emotional and could even be funny. And possibly more important, he taught me that intellectuals did not have to be cold and bookish. Even if they lived with the ancients in their heads half the time, they could be warm and comforting; they could feed you at a time when you needed feeding. He taught me how to roast an eggplant in the fireplace without having it explode. And he taught me how to walk and talk with students when their lives had been changed suddenly by grief.

I sent him this essay a year before he died of cancer, not knowing that he was ill. He wrote me back from Brazil, and it was the last letter I received from him. He wrote, "My eyes are tearing after reading your little sketch of me, out of laughter and joy and something deeper for which I have no words. You are a precious friend, and my heart is singing, here in Campinas, in Brazil, where I feel strangely happy."

Big questions

David Hirsch taught American literature and Judaic studies. His book-cases were overfull and unwieldy, stocked with writers like Melville, Hawthorne, and Poe. He was probably the oldest person on the English faculty at Brown; by the time I met him, he was a professor emeritus. He was tall and stooped, and he had very kind eyes. He also taught a class I signed up for sophomore year called Holocaust Literature.

Professor Hirsch's wife, Roslyn, was a Holocaust survivor and a native Polish speaker; they met when she was a refugee learning English. Together they translated memoirs of Holocaust survivors, narratives from the Kraków Jewish resistance, and stories, almost lost, from the Lodz ghetto.

When I studied with Professor Hirsch in the mid-1990s, postmodernism was the most fashionable lens in most English departments, which made Professor Hirsch unfashionable, with his massive canonical reading lists and courses like the Bible as Literature. He had an intellectual distrust of postmodernism, noting in one of his books that Heidegger had been a Nazi, and that for a philosopher to ignore historical context was very convenient if that philosopher had Nazi ties. He also thought students with postmodernist tendencies had a danger of becoming intellectually lazy; rather than reading *everything*, they could read two or three postmodernist books and interpret everything else using that lens.

"Easier to read two fashionable books," he would say, "than to read *everything*. Takes a lot less time."

When I came to him with an idea for a senior thesis, he kept advising me: *Write something bigger. Ask bigger questions.* When I came to him and told him about my attempt at a full-length play, he was satisfied. He told me that the questions the play was asking were big enough.

Ever since noting that Professor Hirsch was not satisfied with my small questions, I felt emboldened to ask bigger questions. Big unanswerable questions. I now encourage my own students to write plays that contain at least one Big Unanswerable Question. Preferably, I like plays that contain more than one unanswerable question. Sometimes it's frowned upon to ask more than one question at a time in a play. Professor Hirsch and his massive wall of books and his kind eyes made me less afraid of asking more than one question.

I created a class to teach at Yale called Big and Little Plays wherein we read plays of massive scope—in terms of idea, length, or number of characters—and contrast them with plays that employ minimalism. Sometimes the landscape of American theater seems to have shrunk to a midsize car; they fit about five passengers (or characters) and ask one medium-size question. I tend to prefer plays that toggle between an ambitious sprawl and the size of a button. I like the look of thimbles and whales.

Professor Hirsch taught me that if you ask a midsize question you will get a midsize answer. And if you ask a question that is so big it can't really be answered, you can write and read into the great mystery of things, without being easily satisfied.

There has been a death in the family

I found myself on a plane, shouting wildly to the flight attendant in my high school French, "There's been a death in the family, I have to get off. I have to get off this plane." I kept repeating the word *death* in French. The plane was pulling away from the gate, and I was gesticulating wildly, out of my seat. I was on my way from Paris to Germany, where I was hoping to research a play I wanted to write about Oberammergau. I was twenty-one years old, and I wanted desperately to go home.

The flight attendants, beautiful, coiffed, and concerned, eventually told the pilot to bring the plane back to the gate to let me off. I was sobbing and a little shocked at my own assertiveness, as though I had turned into another person, the kind of person who would insist on getting off a plane, inconveniencing hundreds of people. I thanked the flight attendants, ran off the plane, and found a pay phone in the airport. The truth was, I didn't know for sure that there had been a death in the family. But I did *feel strongly* that there had been a death in the family. I called my mother from the pay phone. Sure enough, my grandmother had just died.

This wasn't terribly psychic on my part, in that my grandmother had been sick for a year with lung cancer. It was logical that she would die—but the clarity and force with which I knew in the moment was startling. I booked a ticket home to Chicago; from there, I would drive with my cousin to Iowa for the burial.

My grandmother—my sister and I called her Nanny—was salty. She even put salt on her grapefruit. Her mind was lively and wide. She was often needlepointing while smoking, and watching the television, or listening to the radio, or all three. A child of the Depression, she could never throw anything out. She bought industrial-size sour cream to save money and to feed five children, but by the time I knew her, the kids had all moved out, so the sour cream rotted. It pained her to throw out "a perfectly good" bag, or an empty lipstick container. I'd always loved vintage clothes, and since my grandmother never disposed of anything, it was my good fortune to be able to ransack her closets and wear all her old dresses and coats. My grandmother had an eye for fashion, and we were the same height and size, so I lived in her dresses and in her houndstooth green coat from the 1950s until I wore it out.

When she got diagnosed with lung cancer she said, "Guess I won't be buying any more green bananas." When told to stop smoking, she dismissed the doctor's orders, saying there was a big tumor in there so it probably blocked the smoke from getting to her lungs anyway. She was a philosophical materialist, not fond of organized religion; she told me once that the afterlife made no sense—that if all the bodies went to heaven, the sky would fall down. In order to marry my Irish Catholic grandfather, she had to convert from her Lutheran faith to Catholicism, but she never quite trusted nuns or priests. Without the comfort of belief, she kept her hands busy with needlepoint and her mind busy with books, to forestall despair.

Why was despair often lurking, under her lively exterior? Was it thwarted ambition, her life devoted to being a doctor's wife, or was it just genes from the ancestors—the melancholy Norwegian farmers settled in the landlocked plains of Iowa looking for a sign of the sea where only cornfields billowed? She would disappear to her brother's house in California some summers to be treated by a psychiatrist. She felt she couldn't go to small-town Iowa psychiatrists because they'd discuss her case with her husband, a doctor, as a matter of professional courtesy.

I think it almost killed my grandmother to see my father, her son-in-law, die before her. She walked into the hospital room where he was dying, moaned a deep terrible moan when she saw him, and said, "Nothing to do?!" My grandmother couldn't bear to see youth go before old age. A year later, my grandmother would have cancer.

When she was on her deathbed, my mother asked her, why not forgive her husband for whatever it was that caused a rift. My grandmother said that actually, she'd rather not, because if she forgave him, what a waste of time her anger would have been all those years.

Legend has it that my grandfather wooed my grandmother at the University of Iowa dining hall where he worked as a waiter to put himself through school. He made her a hamburger in the shape of a broken heart, putting ketchup on for blood. Though their marriage seemed to have ossified into a bit of a détente by the time I met them, it was a stable détente. We were all surprised, later, to find passionate love letters between them, saved in an old trunk in the basement. Nanny worried about whether the philandering gene had been passed down to her husband from his father. He had long hours at the hospital, surrounded by nurses, and she didn't like that.

My grandfather's dad had openly carried on with a woman who worked at the local diner in Wellman, Iowa. On the day of my grandparents' wedding, my great-grandfather's mistress shot herself. The day after my grandparents' wedding, the local paper announced their marriage on the front page and, just underneath, the news of the local suicide. Perhaps my grandmother never quite forgave my grandfather for the sins of his father; she felt that the scandal overshadowed her wedding day. I've no idea if her paranoia had any truth to it, or if she was just subject to Othello's "green-eyed monster." She did have beautiful light green eyes, like sea glass.

My grandfather bought her a fancy ring while she was dying. "A little late for that," she coughed.

I *adored* my grandmother. As did her ten grandchildren. She was always ready for a game of Rummikub, and she had a great, full, husky laugh and an ample lap. In fact, I remember her once telling me to sit on her lap when I was far too old, after I'd broken up with my first serious boyfriend.

I was bereft. She told me I was better off without him. She was right, but I started weeping.

"Come, sit on my lap," she said.

"I'm too old!" I said. (I was twenty-one.)

"Come on, sit on my lap!" And she held me and rocked me in that old breakfast nook while I sniffled.

After her death, my cousin and I drove from Chicago to Iowa to meet the rest of the family for the funeral. I was jet-lagged. We passed the endless cornfields in silence. Red barns rose up from the mist. Signs for PEACE ROAD in Illinois let us know we would soon cross the Mississippi River to Iowa. I had always been terrified, as a child in the passenger seat, to drive over the bridge between Illinois and Iowa. That massive steel bridge hangs over the Mississippi River, and I would imagine, as a child, tumbling out and drowning. My cousin and I crossed the bridge and talked about our grandmother.

All her life, my grandmother kept busy. Book club, Tuesday club, Wednesday club, literary club, bridge club, cribbage, fishing, bowling . . . She read constantly, and believed that books were the way to know the self and the other. She prized wisdom over cleverness. At the age of seventy she was reading Audre Lorde for the first time. I often wonder what her life would have been like if she had used her social work degree for something other than being the president of the ladies' auxiliary committee for doctors' wives. She was always deeply *interested*.

I think if I were to ask my grandmother what the secret of life was, she would tell me that it was to be always and forever *interested*, deeply interested in other people and the world. She would tell me that the bonds of family are more important than momentary anger, that women can and should write down everything they see, and that, when making mashed potatoes, you do not need to choose between butter, sour cream, and cream cheese. Put in all three.

How to drop out of graduate school

First, be sure to pick a graduate school that is insanely expensive, located in a ridiculously unaffordable city, in a profession that gives you few if any guaranteed prospects postgraduation and loans that you have no idea how you're going to pay for. That's what I did, anyway.

I arrived on time to the first day of class, looking around at the other anxious faces of fellow students. I waited. The teacher was late. I waited some more. Inside my head, I sang a little dirge about money and loans to the tune of *How am I going to pay for this?*

I waited for another hour; but still, the professor did not come. Later that day, on a tour of the campus, the tour guide told us that though this particular MFA program just started and has very few production opportunities for playwrights, it would continue to grow, and isn't it wonderful to get in on the ground floor of this exciting new beginning?

I called my mentor, Paula Vogel. She told me to drop out, that she hadn't told me earlier because I seemed so excited to move to that ridiculously expensive city.

I called the dean to tell her I was dropping out before signing my loan papers. She told me that I hadn't really experienced the program yet because my professor didn't show up to the first class. "Just go to your first class and see how you feel," she said in a very plummy English accent (she taught voice).

I went to the next class. This time the professor showed up. He looked at me with his powerful, intense gaze, and in front of the class said, "What's the deal? I hear you're thinking of dropping out?"

I stammered something about how I'd rather talk about this outside of class. He continued to interrogate me about why I called the dean to say I might drop out. The other playwrights turned to look at me and my face got hot. "Are you staying or going?" he asked. I demurred, and class began. He instructed us, "Put your head on the desk and look at the light inside your body." The whole class, including me, dutifully put our heads on the desk and closed our eyes. After about a half hour with my head on the desk, I picked up my head to look around and stretch, but he put his hand on my head and steered it back on the desk. I started to hear the little dirge again, this song about how much this all costs, as I tried to look at the light inside my body. At the end of the exercise, he asked everyone to come up with a word about how they felt while looking at the light inside their bodies. Some said *peaceful*; some said *sad*.

Then it was my turn and I said *crown*, because I saw a little crown of light there, right near my heart.

"Crown is not a feeling," he said, irritated. "You need a feeling for this exercise."

"Crowned?" I said, earnestly trying.

He looked irritated again and said, "'Crowned' is not a feeling. Happy. Happy is your feeling."

And I thought, *Happy is not my feeling. Happy is really not my feeling right now.* And as I tried to freewrite from a made-up character's happy point of view, I thought: *I am not happy, and I am dropping out of this institution after this class.*

But first, we all had to go around and read what we wrote. The professor listened, stopping us when he felt we had stopped writing authentically. Somehow, though he had just met us, he knew when we were engaged in a true creative authentic flow and when we started writing self-consciously, without reference to the light inside our bodies.

I dropped out officially that afternoon. I hadn't signed any loan papers yet, so that part was good. No one from the department called me to see why I dropped out. And it took the bureaucracy at least two months to catch up and kick me out of student housing. By that time, I had five or so part-time jobs to stay afloat. My actress housemate sold my grandmother's vintage coats to an East Village junk shop for pocket change. I asked for the coats back, then moved down the block, out of student housing. My friends helped carry my futon, books, and crappy lamp down the street like a little parade.

I saw as much theater in that ridiculously expensive town as I could manage that year. Had some torrid affairs, drank a little bit too much some nights. I made up writing deadlines with my best and, let's face it, only friend, fellow playwright Andy Bragen. We made up little punishments for each other when we didn't meet our writing deadlines. I made up a punishment for Andy; he had to do the Jane Fonda workout in his sweatpants while I watched in his East Village apartment. I taught English at Berlitz language school, and felt immensely grateful when an old friend with a good job took me out for a big chicken dinner on Easter and insisted on paying. I ate as much hot-and-sour soup with a side of rice from the Chinese restaurant on the corner as I could; it was only a buck fifty and covered two meals. I never wanted to eat hot-and-sour soup again after that year, but I felt a deep sense of joy and liberation that I finally managed to do something scholastically irresponsible after all those years on the planet as a model student.

That spring, I applied to a different graduate school that was subsidized, and where the professors showed up to their classes. And I left that ridiculously expensive city until one day I returned, with a little more knowledge and therefore power.

Tina Howe and the pink elephant

After I dropped out of graduate school, one of the first people I called for advice was the playwright Tina Howe. I had grown up reading Tina's groundbreaking plays. Some absurdist, surreal comedies about motherhood; others formally inventive plays about her blue-blood family. My dear playwright friend Andy had studied with Tina in college and encouraged me to reach out to her. I was nervous to speak to a literary hero and thanked Tina profusely for speaking with me over the phone. I told her that I was a recent graduate school dropout.

She said (and I am paraphrasing), "Oh, that's wonderful! When I was your age no one went to playwriting school! We just *lived*. Sam Shepard, Ntozake Shange, we all lived and wrote and went to Paris and smoked pot and no one went to school."

She said, "Everything I learned, I learned from reading and seeing the plays of Ionesco. Don't worry, just live in New York City, see as much theater as possible, and keep writing."

I followed her advice that year. On some level, I think I didn't know a person could just *move* to New York City from the Midwest and *live*, without attaching a degree to the whole situation. It was a liberation.

When, four years later, I had my first play produced in New York City, downtown for three nights at the wonderful tiny Ohio Theatre, produced by Clubbed Thumb, there was Tina, with a pink crystal Ganesha elephant in her hands that she handed me as a present. (I now take that Ganesha with me to every opening.) Tina was tall and slim, with white hair that was always combed neatly around her ears, and she was usually swathed in some kind of extraordinary tunic or robe with flamboyant patterns— something that gave the impression of wings. When I wrote a play with a bird in it, she gave me earrings with little feathers inside a glass dome;

she probably had a pair herself. She was a fabulist, and she always looked fabulous.

At The Dramatist Guild, we did a panel together and I complimented her on her seashell necklace, and she said, "You want it? You can have it!" and undid the clasp. Out of the corner of my eye, after the panel, I saw that her husband, Norman, looked pained; it turned out he'd given her the seashell necklace. I tried to refuse the gift, but she sent it to me later through the mail, beautifully wrapped. I learned to be careful of complimenting Tina on any jewelry or clothes.

Tina has been at every single play I've ever had in New York City, calming my nerves, giving me buoyancy during the stressful time of previews. After I had babies, she would stop by and comfort me through the anxiety of wondering if I'd ever balance writing and mothering. She would say, "I used to write at the dining room table after dropping the kids at school. At two p.m., an internal alarm would go off, and I would know it was time to stop writing and pick them up. No one wants to write more than five hours a day anyway, so it's a perfect schedule." And she added, "When they're babies, just roll around with them on the floor, don't even try to write, it goes so fast."

I tried to follow her advice. Years later, when I myself was a teacher, I realized that she had no reason to speak to me that first time on the phone but for kindness—she was not formally my teacher in any way, she had no obligation to give me advice or comfort.

Over the past ten years, she cared tirelessly for her husband, who had a long, arduous siege of Alzheimer's. As things took a downward turn, I visited them as much as possible. The last time I stopped by the Upper West Side apartment that Tina and Norman shared, I heard Tina through the door:

"There's been a shit show! Just a giant shit show! Norman did the most enormous shit—it went into his *socks*; it went everywhere, through the diaper on the bed in the hallway—"

I walked in and heard Norman moaning in the bathroom.

Tina and I cleaned up together. As she flew through the apartment cleaning, she shouted, "I'll be there in a second—Wasn't that the most *impressive* shit—Did you see that's a photograph of me and Ionesco, I revered him; and he liked me too, and do you see how many hands are there in that photograph? Are there four hands, or five? Five! Yes! An extra hand in the background—I'm so glad you noticed."

She settled Norman into a chair, brought him crackers and water, and started what seemed to be a familiar litany.

"Where did we meet, Norman?" she asked.

"Arthur Loeb's house," he answered.

"And what was I wearing?"

"A red dress."

"Yes, but I had no breasts, and so I covered up the décolletage with my hands and Norman said, 'Either wear it or take it off!' Norman, who is the cutest?"

"You are."

"No, you are."

Then Norman fell asleep in his chair and Tina told me, "I'm still ambitious, I still want to write, I want to write about unexplored terrain, women are still an undiscovered country."

A month later, they moved into an assisted-living facility together. It was physically too hard for Tina to care for Norman anymore. Three weeks after they arrived, Norman died. After sixty years of marriage.

I visited Tina in her new domicile. She told me that she was making friends but that it was lonely. She was having trouble with her own memory now. She worried that she may have caught dementia from caring for her husband. She was trying to write a series of one-acts, called *Where Women Go*.

Before she moved, while she was downsizing, she gave me some of the books in her collection—some of them first editions. Then she insisted that I take home the dollhouse she'd had built with a replica of Paris inside. She showed me the extraordinary object. "The lights go on inside!" she said, turning on a switch. "There is the Pont Neuf. There's the Seine!"

Indeed, she'd asked a set designer to build a miniature Paris for her in the dollhouse.

"Take it home," said Tina, "you'll see, your children will disappear inside of it and go to Paris for the whole afternoon."

Once, Tina came to see my play *Letters from Max* at the Signature Theatre, and we had lunch with a large group of playwrights beforehand. When I asked her what's new, she said, "What's new in my world is that everything is very much the same," adding that "Things collapse over time into strange new configurations."

She said that she wasn't interested in writing anymore but that she saw it as her duty to cheer up all the widows at the retirement home where she lived. She said that because men die statistically before women, there were too many sad widows. And then she said, "I've decided my new job is to be kind and helpful to the people at the home instead of being upset that I'm there. I meet a newcomer, almost always a widow, and I say, you might be homesick but buck up, we have good entertainment here."

I asked her how she was able to be such a generous teacher and she said, "I think teaching is about generosity, about wanting to give and to be kind. I never had any training to be a teacher. I knew how to write plays, but I didn't know how to teach. Suddenly, when my plays were being done, I was in a position to help other people get their plays done. And now I'm an elder statesman. I have a perch. The only way out, the only key—is to be generous. Be generous if you can."

I thought about that phrase for a long time: *be generous if you can.* Not just *be generous*, but *if you can.* Tina seemed to be pointing to the fact that generosity was a privilege, a practice and an ability, that certain conditions had to be met to allow generosity to flower. I am by no means the only recipient of Tina's generosity; she raised a generation of playwrights. In fact, a playwright friend who had studied with Tina recently told me she was considering getting a tattoo of Tina's advice to her: "Embed the miraculous in the most unlikely places."

On that day at lunch, Tina had a beautifully wrapped gift for me, and for everyone else at the table; she gave all the playwrights at the table PEZ dispensers that she'd been able to get at the drugstore a short walking distance from her assisted-living facility. And journals, to write in.

Tina died in August, a year and a month after Norman died. She'd had a fall, broken her hip, and died of complications post-surgery. When I last visited her, I'd brought her a little blue journal, and she was chagrined that she didn't have a gift for me. She'd been banned from walking to the drugstore by herself, because she'd gotten lost.

"I must have a gift for you! I know I have a gift for you!" she said, moving quickly around her room. "Ah! I've found the perfect thing," she said. "I made this!" She gave me a little wooden box that she'd painted in a class at the nursing home. She'd painted it red, blue, and yellow and glued on a photograph, torn from a magazine, of a hot-air balloon, and framed the photo with golden pipe cleaners. It was perfect. A hot-air balloon box from Tina, always floating, hiding treasure. She's always understood the power and magic of opening a gift, of a gift passing from one hand to another.

And when I think of Tina now, I reflect that we remember what we are given more than we remember what we gave away, if the gift was freely given.

See one, do one, teach one

My grandfather did not want to die. He was eighty-four and had lived a good life as a devoted pediatrician in Davenport, Iowa. He'd had five children and ten grandchildren. He grew up in the Depression as a child in an even smaller Iowa town with an outhouse; he ended up owning a house with multiple bathrooms. As a child, he was sometimes driven by hunger to shoot squirrels for food in Wellman, Iowa, and he went on able to provide deep metal bins of buttery popcorn for his children. He helped to test the polio vaccine in Iowa and had personally treated most of the families and children in Davenport—the mumps, rubella, meningitis—I still run into people whose lives he saved.

My mother called my grandfather first with any pediatric question, and he was always a source of calm. Once, while changing my sister's diaper, my mom impaled my sister with a diaper pin; my mom called her dad in a panic, and he talked her down.

I learned the medical training mantra from my grandfather: "See one, do one, teach one." The phrase refers to an intern (or doctor in training) watching a procedure, then doing a procedure, then, finally, teaching—passing along the knowledge to the next generation of doctors. I loved the idea that the learning was only complete once a doctor had taught what they'd learned. A sealing in of knowledge by teaching—a kind of surgical circle of life.

My grandfather had had leukemia for three years by the time he was on his deathbed. Every time his breath seemed impossibly ragged, and probably his last, my mother, uncles, aunts, and I would gather round the hospital bed and hold him, sing to him, touch him, and his breathing would even out, his heart rate thundering back to normal. My uncles re-told him family stories since he couldn't speak. At one point, one of my uncles recited cribbage scores to him, inducing a meditative calm. We held vigil like that for three days. My aunt rubbed his feet, saying they'd probably never been touched before, certainly not by his wife.

I wondered if my grandfather was afraid to die, or if he simply fought death out of habit. Maybe he felt he had more living to do. I wondered if, from a doctor's point of view, death seemed like a bit of a defeat. He went to Catholic Mass every Sunday. Did he have repentance on his mind? Did he think he'd find my grandmother again in heaven, and would she still be angry with him there? She'd died of cancer on his seventy-fourth birthday, which always seemed a bit of a punishment.

My grandfather looked a little bit like Wilford Brimley in the Quaker Oats commercials, and indeed, he ate Quaker Oats every morning, proclaiming the advantages of oatmeal for staying regular. He also extolled the virtues of the anus; he once said that calling someone an asshole as an insult was ridiculous, because an asshole was a very fine organ, capable of distinguishing between air, solid, and liquid. *Wasn't that amazing?* he said, *a fine organ, the asshole.* He was a creature of habit. Oatmeal in the morning, gin at night, church on Sundays, a steady dose of ministering to the sick, railing about politics, and watching football in between. When he yawned, he made this noise: *Hee, hee hum.* He was a man who wore a hat. He did not travel all that much but kept a large map on the wall, with pushpins that marked all the spots where his family had traveled. Stolid, solid, he rarely praised his children, saying: "He who wishes to make men mad first praises them."

When he was in his late seventies, he saw one of my early plays in Chicago. He told me two things: First, "I'm proud of you." Second: "Next time, maybe you should try writing a comedy." I wondered if he saved his expressions of pride for his grandchildren, skipping over his children, softening in his old age, assuming he wouldn't ruin us with a bit of praise.

He never did see one of my comedies. He finally died after that long vigil in the Iowa Catholic hospital, where morphine was monitored very carefully (God forbid the family should be accused of helping things along). It did not matter how many Masses my grandfather had attended as a form of religious preparation—that man did not want to die. I wondered what kind of softening, beyond religious piety, prepared one for death. Why had my father let go more easily, at the age of fifty-three, than my grandfather had, at the age of eighty-four? My grandfather clung to life as fiercely as any soldier on the field of battle. His frame was *solid*. But he eventually shuddered into the next world.

His brick family house (also a solid frame) was sold shortly thereafter. I miss that house and dream of it often. The house was both metaphor and reality—an actual gathering spot, and a site of possibility and memory. Years later, I visited the house with my aunt and uncle; we asked to come in. The new owner let us in to look around. The floor plan was the same, but the mantel where my grandfather had hung all his hats was now a gun rack. I hated that his hats had been transformed into guns. My grandfather's hat rack represented, for me, a time when grown men wore hats. A time when men wanted to look like grown-ups in fedoras rather than looking like teenagers in baseball caps. A time when I could come home, and home was self-evident—a word, a memory, a place.

See one, do one, teach one.

When I was a child, I watched my grandfather fry an egg. First, he would test the egg to make sure it wasn't rotten. With my grandmother's habit of saving large cartons of food past expiration date, he had to employ the scientific method. He taught me that you could drop an egg in a bowl of water: the good ones sank; the bad ones, full of gas, floated. Then, good egg in hand, you heat up a pan with some butter (olive oil does not produce the same crisp fried edges); crack the egg into the pan, watch, and wait. After a couple minutes, you put a lid on the pan to hold the steam, and produce a thin film on the yoke for dunking perfection. How many times have I fried an egg since my grandfather died? Countless. And there he is.

I have passed on to my children my knowledge of the sunny-side up egg. I hope I have also learned the art of testing eggs from my grandfather—the floaters, the sinkers, the keepers. The ones you hold on to for dear life.

Gifts

After I finished my graduate program in creative writing, I found myself suddenly without health insurance and with a kidney infection, otherwise known as pyelonephritis. I felt awful, and I must have looked awful, because my former teacher Paula Vogel took one look at my gray face and insisted that I go to her doctor.

"But I don't have insurance," I said.

She slid a check for five hundred dollars under my door so that I could get treatment.

Paula told me not to pay the money back but to give it to another young artist in trouble when I started making money from writing plays. I said I couldn't possibly. She said that five hundred dollars was given to her by an older woman when her partner had health issues in her early twenties and they couldn't afford health care. She said that her benefactor told her not to repay the loan but to recirculate it instead.

It was only through the power of Paula's story about gifts that I allowed myself to receive her gift and go to her doctor. The story, then, was part of the gift.

Lewis Hyde wrote in his beautiful and seminal book *The Gift*, "A gift that cannot be given away ceases to be a gift." *The Gift* is an incredible teaching about how to reorient yourself as an artist inside an economy that doesn't always seem to care about artists; in other words, he writes that making art fits into a gift economy, even when we're also situated within a capitalist economy that turns art into merchandise to be bought and sold.

I often begin the semester teaching playwrights by having them read *The Gift*. And then I have them write short "gift plays" to each other. I ask them to interview one another, then write short plays specifically made for one another, that never get seen by anyone else. I want to remind them that writing does not have to be an act of solipsistic catharsis; it can be a gift-giving instead. Crucially, Hyde talks about nonreciprocal gifts that keep on moving through the culture. In other words, if you give me a gift on a particular holiday, so I also give you a gift, the loop is closed. Instead, Hyde talks about gifts that are passed on and on, because they are not situated only between two people. The closest we get to this concept in America is the phrase "Pay it forward."

Interestingly, some of the most successful plays have been gifts. *The Mousetrap*, the longest running play in London, was a gift Agatha Christie gave to her grandson. She bestowed the royalties of that particular play on him when he was a child, before she was a worldwide sensation, and though he says at the time he remembered her present of the red bicycle more vividly, the play would go on to earn millions of dollars for him, much of which he's given to charity. *Long Day's Journey into Night* was a gift Eugene O'Neill gave to his wife Carlotta on their twelfth wedding anniversary, writing, "Dearest, I give you the original script of this play of old sorrow, written in tears and blood." She published it three years after his death. And the money it has earned continues to support young playwrights, through O'Neill's charitable foundations.

I do not mean to harp on the economic boon of some singularly successful gift plays; the spiritual nature of gift plays are equally important. I believe that every work of art that begins with a dedication is a gift, to a private someone, before it makes its way into the world. Bach ended almost every piece of music with this dedication: "To God alone, the glory."

And Paula Vogel's five hundred dollars has flown about the world in various ways. I have no idea where it landed—and I hope I never do—I hope it just keeps going.

María Irene Fornés on pleasure and the moment

In my early twenties I studied with the great teacher and playwright María Irene Fornés. I met her at a writing workshop in Taxco, Mexico. A venerated painter from Cuba, she turned to playwriting later in life and became one of the most important voices of her generation. She was also too often overlooked, even as she shaped the next generation of playwrights.

When I met her, she was in her late sixties, and in the early stages of Alzheimer's, but all of her students back then just thought she was an iconic artist who occasionally forgot her keys. As she continued to lose her memory, she had to remind herself that she was a writer; to keep writing, she wrote on scraps of paper the word *write* and taped them to the wall. If I ever need a lesson about duration, or resilience, I can just imagine that little piece of paper scrawled with her handwriting: *write.*

When I was twenty-three, I got into a crowded taxi with Irene in Mexico; we were all going out for dinner, and there wasn't really room for me, but Irene said, "Come on, sit on my lap, I'll be your seat belt." That Irene was once my seat belt somehow gives me courage for the rest of my writing life.

In that workshop, she taught me that in many American acting schools, actors are taught they must always want something from someone else, and often there is an obstacle to their character getting what they want. Playwrights are traditionally taught to write scenes that way—as schematic maps of thwarted desire. Fornés found this tedious. She said in that workshop, "Who wants something from someone else all the time? Only criminals, and Americans."

She went on to say, "American actors are taught to have objectives— what your character wants from another character, etc. That is *business.*

When I deal with other people, I don't *want* something from them. I want a rapport. Some people say that's an objective—it's not—it's a sensation of well-being. . . . Life is not about constantly wanting to get something from someone else. Life is about pleasure." There is plenty of desire in Fornés's work, but she describes desire differently from the language of having a simple "objective" or "want."

One might ask, how is desire different from having an objective? And what moves us to pleasure if not an aim, a will? Even as children, without language, we must point to a bowl of berries in order to eat them, to experience pleasure. How to describe human behavior in a drama without this sense of drive and will?

Fornés said she started writing plays after she saw Beckett's *Waiting for Godot* in Paris, and Fornés thought Beckett described life accurately. She turned more and more from painting to writing, and Susan Sontag, her lover, encouraged her. She taught us that rather than fixating on a character's thwarted objectives, what the character wanted to do, in the future—we must focus on the moment. She took acting classes with Lee Strasberg to better understand theater. She told my friend Michelle Memran, who made a brilliant documentary (*The Rest I Make Up*) about Irene, "Moment to moment . . . moment to moment . . . I have never once in writing a play given a thought about what the scene's about or what I want to say to the audience. . . . The audience isn't there when I'm writing a play."

She managed to teach her students creative process, a very hard thing to do, to take your students inside process itself, rather than commenting on their artistic products. When I studied with Irene, she would rarely even read our work. That just wasn't where her teaching lived, at least not when I met her. The teaching lived in a sacred moment prior to the writing—she was trying to teach the divine spark. She would have us close our eyes, envision scenes, do yoga exercises, meditate. The writing was the icing on the cake. Irene taught us that anything that an artist can make interesting onstage is drama. She said that even an event that might seem boring—like a puddle expanding on a road—can be interesting if we make it so.

I remember once having lunch with Irene in the West Village, where she lived for a long time. I told her about my new play *The Clean House.* I told her I wanted to start the play with a joke in Portuguese, a language many people in an American audience might not understand, because I wanted to see if a joke could be funny beyond language.

Irene looked and me and said, "But that's stupid! How will the joke be funny if no one can understand the joke?" Irene did not mince words.

She also taught us not to treat our characters like puppets. She would say nothing is more annoying than controlling parents at a dinner party who tell their children what to say—*Say hello to Mister So-and-So*—in a prating voice. No, she would say. Let your characters speak to you, and listen carefully to them, and write down what they say. She was, in effect, teaching us spontaneity, improvisation, a Virginia Woolf-like insistence on being fully with and in the moment while it passes. Just as Fornés didn't want her actors thinking of the future while playing her scenes, she didn't want her student writers planning out their plays, or thinking about where their plays were going with an aim, directive, or argument. An outline? God forbid. She wanted us to surprise ourselves in the act of writing and life. Apparently she once taught Susan Sontag, who was then having a hard time writing, how easy it is to write by sitting at the kitchen table and using prompts by opening cookbooks and randomly borrowing their phraseology for starting points. She taught countless writers the art of spontaneity.

When I visited Irene in a nursing home by the time she was deep in dementia, she seemed to have no wants. I pushed her in her wheelchair, saying, "Do you want to go see the birds? Or should we go in the other direction?" She didn't answer. I hoped that the simple act of being together was enough for her, as it was for so many of her characters, suspended in a state of grace, or communion.

Irene died of Alzheimer's in that nursing home in 2018, after a grueling decade, in which she was moved from nursing home to nursing home, sustained by a small cadre of theater-as-chosen-family like Michelle, who cared for her at the end. The conscience of the broader theater community was awakened late—the idea that a respected elder such as Irene, a master teacher and practitioner of the form, could die alone and forgotten—was reprehensible. Michelle, Michelle's partner, and a dear friend washed Irene's body moments after she died, changed Irene out of her hospital gown and into a clean shirt, and brushed her hair.

I hold the memory of Irene close when I feel trapped by any "should" states of mind about the writing of a play. And her observations are instructive not only in the theater but also in life:

· Do not always want something from someone else.
· Do not be fooled into thinking that violence or conflict is the only drama to pay attention to.
· Don't tell other people what to say.
· Life is about pleasure.
· Do what you love until you die.

Two

Branches

There is no cure for
yearning. Even the trees bend
in the wind like that.

Lessons from a marriage

I could lie and say the reason I can write and have three kids is sheer force of will or my excellent time-management skills. It's neither. It's because I married a feminist. I am now going to issue a warning. If you are annoyed with your husband, wife, or partner right now, don't read this. If you are a single mother, tell me to shut up. If you are slightly annoyed with the division of labor in your household and are looking for other models, you might read this, but, also, forgive me.

Before he was my husband, he was my housemate named Tony. Tony was largely raised by a single mother who had been a midwife. He learned from his mother about women, work, and survival. And because I lived with him before I started dating him, I was able to casually notice early on that he liked cooking. He liked sweeping. He liked watering the plants, and ironing. I thought . . . *Hmmm* . . . *that is very sexy, watering plants and ironing*. After all, watering plants is the original definition of *husbandry*. Tony's mentor in college happened to be a feminist biologist, Anne Fausto-Sterling, who is married to my mentor, the playwright Paula Vogel. Tony learned from his mentor about how the scientific world is gendered, and how to live with a playwright. Apparently, it's not easy to live with a playwright. Our thoughts are often elsewhere.

When I was walking down the street recently with my daughters in Brooklyn, a woman admired my daughter's complicated fishtail braids.

"Who did those braids?" she asked.

"My husband," I said.

She gasped.

I learned from watching Tony braid. I watched his precision and patience. Both firm and gentle, he gathered up three strands, making them one. It was a perfect metaphor for the making of our family. Our three children—the strands separate, but also three parts becoming one.

When we had twins, Tony developed good systems of bottle-feeding the babies simultaneously at night. He put them each in a bouncy chair, sat between them, and administered two bottles. He saw that I was exhausted and overwhelmed and started making meal plans and grocery lists for the week. This kind of domestic planning makes my head hurt. I tend to buy groceries when I notice we need them. Like when there is suddenly no milk for my tea. It is slightly pathetic. I need tea in order to write, and I need milk in my tea, so when I notice I am not writing because there is no milk in my tea it occurs to me that we are out of groceries. This might be a slight exaggeration. *Good Housekeeping* once wanted to give me an award of some kind, which Tony found hilarious.

I will say that our division of labor was not always easy to figure out. It required and requires constant refinement. It was hard-won. There were many conversations, some heated. And tears.

I remember when my daughter was in elementary school and she asked Tony, "Why do you never pick us up from school?"

He answered, "Because I have a job."

My daughter answered, "But Mom has a job too, and she picks us up from school."

My husband thought about this and rearranged his work schedule to pick her up the following Monday.

When we were deciding about whether to have a bigger family, I told Tony I couldn't imagine having more children if he wasn't home more often. So he altered his schedule (he is a child psychiatrist) so that he could be home more often. When I was knee-deep in rehearsal one year, Tony noticed that I dropped the ball making playdates for the kids, so he just took it over. He found that he was better at scheduling than I was, so he kept doing it.

I read somewhere that Joan Didion's husband woke up, made

breakfast for their daughter, then took her to school. Then Joan Didion would wake up, stretch, drink a Diet Coke in bed, and start writing. Our morning routine is not quite like this. But I tend to stumble around in a fog in the morning, while Tony makes breakfast. He used to slip a poem into Anna's lunchbox, too, as some kind of spiritual recompense for her having celiac disease and not being able to eat in the hot food line.

I was recently at dinner and told my friends (a couple) that I was working on an essay about why I married a feminist, and my friends started to ask questions about the division of labor in my household. I began telling what chores Tony does and it immediately produced friction between a happy husband and wife.

The husband said, "Sarah, couldn't you at least have put the poem in the children's lunch? Isn't that sort of your department?"

I felt guilty.

The wife said, "Sarah, haven't you heard that blues song, 'Don't Advertise Your Man'?"

I hadn't. Then the husband started asking the wife what domestic things he did that she appreciated, and there was a long pause and I thought, *I better change the subject.* I hadn't even gotten to the part where Tony learned to use an Instant Pot.

The truth is, Tony enjoys doing many of these tasks. He finds some relief and transcendence in ordering chaos. That dynamic is particular to our two temperaments and not applicable to gender relations in general. But I do wonder: If we can find nurturing and domestic competence in a man sexy, could that transform the division of household labor? What if men felt that excellently dispatched domestic labor made them desirable, made them a catch? *I want you so bad when you make lunch for the kids. Meet me around the corner after drop-off.*

Tony and I did not ourselves get married until we saw our mentors get married. We watched Anne and Paula get married in Massachusetts, soon after the laws on gay marriage changed in that state. Then two years later, we asked them to get frocked for the day, and one November day in California, they married us. Being married by two women who had a healthy distrust of marriage-as-institution because of its patriarchal history was helpful, I think, in setting a certain tone.

I think an equal marriage is many things to many people. But for me, equal parenting is when you worry the same amount but on different days; not only taking the children to the doctor the same amount, but also making the appointments, and a healthy distribution of worry when they are sick. I once heard Gloria Steinem say, "Yes, women can have it all, a career and a baby, but not until men do too. What I mean is, not until men are equal parents."

An equal marriage also values different kinds of work, regardless of economics. When we were first cohabiting and I earned very little money from my writing, Tony never thought my writing time should be equated with its earning potential. Valuing different kinds of work is vital. An equal marriage is not just about the distribution of chores but equal thinking about chores. Reading that last sentence, I think I just failed according to my own definition of an equal marriage.

I don't want you to think I am describing a seamless partnership, or one without conflict. Tony and I have plenty of quarrels. We fight about where to put a chair. And about how many books is right to have in a New York apartment (as many as possible, obviously); whether overhead lighting is better than lamps (lamps, clearly); and how to organize mittens (is that even a thing?).

Some fights begin with a proposal of mine, and Tony's response, "That is not a very practical idea." When we fight, sometimes I write him a poem the next day to make up to him. But I think secretly he might rather have me take out the garbage more often than write him a poem.

He said to me once, "Love is not romantic. Only romance is romantic. And romances end."

And then I asked, "But doesn't that mean love doesn't have to end but romances do? Isn't that kind of romantic?"

I myself am a romantic. So I try to find his anti-romantic posturing kind of romantic. Plus, he is secretly romantic. For example, when I turned forty, he blindfolded me and put me in a taxi. We drove to Williamsburg, Brooklyn, to a terrarium shop. I'd never seen a terrarium in my life, never even knew the word. When we got to the shop, Tony took the blindfold off me and I saw all of that lovely green foliage under domes of glass. Moss, succulents, and the green shoots of spring. I wanted to inhale all that green light. We made terrariums together that afternoon and then tried to keep them. Tony must have felt like I'd have a better chance keeping alive succulents under glass; they are hard to kill and you just have to spray them with water occasionally. Tony is better at keeping plants alive than I am—no surprise there.

Tony and I both dislike conflict and had to learn to fight early on. His view of marriage initially was apocalyptic, as his parents' marriage he grew up observing as a child was an explosive one that ended with quite a bit of collateral damage. He taught a class at NYU for a decade called Children of Divorce, one he was uniquely qualified to teach, as both a child psychiatrist and a child of divorce. Sometimes our dinner guests would look at our bookcases and seem slightly alarmed when they would see huge stacks with *divorce* in the titles. One of Tony's assignments was for his students to do an oral history of their parents' relationships and views on love; he would teach his students how to effectively fight with their partners, showing them a Monty Python clip about the nature of argument. And yet even experts on fighting can have blind spots at home.

For example, we have a long-standing fight about clearing the table. Tony likes to sit and talk after a meal, and I like to jump up and clear the dishes as soon as I'm done eating. When I get up to do the dishes and no one else leaps up to help, it irritates me. And when I jump up to do the dishes while people are still relaxing post-meal and talking, it annoys

Tony. Writing it down, the fight seems petty, and yet, we have gone back and forth, back and forth about this, over *years*. When I clear and wash the dishes while everyone is still talking over the dinner table, I suddenly feel like my grandmother, put upon, and then I get mad, banging around dishes in the sink. But Tony says no one is asking me to jump up and do the dishes. That if I just waited, they would all help. For some reason, I never believe it. I believe they will drift off to do Wordle on their phones.

Recently, after yet another heated argument about dish washing, how and when to do it, Tony told me that, as a psychiatrist, all day long he listens to other people's suffering, and that dinner is the one time during the day he has reciprocal conversation. Therefore, he does not want dinner to end prematurely. He wants it to go on and on until it can't go on anymore. I didn't know that.

"How could you not have known that?" he asked.

"You didn't tell me," I said. All at once I understood that what I thought was a fight about gender roles was, in his mind, a fight about how to be a family together after a solitary day.

The following night I sat at the table until everyone was truly done eating, digesting, and talking. And I tried to remember Thich Nhat Hanh's instructions on how to wash dishes. He counsels the reader to wash dishes as though you are washing a baby in the sink, with that much care. Sometimes washing dishes is about the division of labor, but sometimes washing dishes is about the spiritual life.

I learn how to be married every day.

Beth Henley and luck

The great playwright Beth Henley, a dear friend, said to me not long after her mother was murdered in Mississippi, "I'm so lucky, because the murderer pled guilty, so we won't have to go to trial."

Beth is always looking for hope or luck in the darkest of places. Her mother had been murdered in Mississippi; her nephew had also been murdered in Mississippi, six years prior. After these tragedies, Beth raised her son as a single mother, and she carried on writing. She said she wrote a comedy after her mother was murdered, to see if she could still make herself laugh.

I met Beth at a writers' retreat when I was in my early twenties. I'd hardly had a play produced, and Beth was a revered figure, author of the Pulitzer Prize–winning *Crimes of the Heart*. When I first saw her, she was wearing a big floppy hat and sitting cross-legged on a lawn, writing. We struck up a friendship, and when I moved to Los Angeles, where my future husband did his medical residency, almost never home, Beth was one of my only friends.

It's hard to make friends in Los Angeles, especially if you've moved there dragging your feet, for love. I hated the place at first; resented the sunlight, which made every day feel the same. I felt my memory was being highjacked; my memory was tied to the smell of the seasons changing, I reasoned, so I could hardly remember what I did one week to the next.

Maybe I couldn't remember what I did one week to the next because I had very few friends, and my solitary life consisted mostly of going to the local coffee shop to write, while my beloved looked after people traumatized by violence at the veterans hospital all day and often all through the night.

When I was lonely, or hopeless about the writing life, I would call Beth, and she would take me out and make me laugh. When Tony and I got engaged, on Saint Patrick's Day, we went to Beth's Saint Paddy's party that night and showed off our three-dollar three-metal rings we'd bought each other by the beach.

When I first got pregnant, Tony had a day of existential dread about bringing a child into this universe that seemed so grim so much of the time. I can't remember what awful thing had happened that week in the news, but it was during the war in Iraq. Tony had driven home from the veterans hospital listening to the radio, thinking, *The world can be such an awful place.* He feared bringing a baby into such a world.

When he got home, Beth was at our apartment, and we were having tea. Tony asked Beth how, as someone touched by violence, she maintained optimism about the world.

Beth said that every day she woke up and thought: *I might see something beautiful today. I might wake up and see a poem, or a sunset, or my kid might say something funny. And that's enough, despite the degradations of the world. That every day you wake up, you might see something beautiful.*

I remember, the morning I went into labor with Anna, Tony put on a nice shirt and jacket to go to the hospital with me.

"Why are you getting dressed up?" I said, heaving and puffing. But I knew. It was an act of optimism, a ritual of faith, guarding against chaos, while bringing a baby into a world full of trouble.

Dr. Seuss and Virginia Woolf, or letter to my daughters

Dear Daughters,

You, my girls, are the unapologetic generation. At the moment I write you this letter, you are nine and thirteen, and for years and years, before you were born, women's whole lives were one big apology. You will grow up, and I hope you will apologize only when you did something wrong.

I can feel it already, when I meet the upcoming generation, this lack of apology around the eyes. Sometimes I find it disconcerting. Sometimes I even take it, at first, for rudeness. Then I realize there is a direct quality, a quality that eschews original sin. A straightforward "Hello, nice to meet you, I have done nothing wrong. And who are you?"

I hope I can learn from you and your generation, and what your generation knows just by growing up in a changed culture, and not just imagining one to come. I hope that you will have lots of new "of courses" that I didn't have when I was a girl. Of course women can be president. (Please, God.) Of course there are movies where women are superheroes. Of course women can marry women and men can marry men. Of course gender is not a fixed binary. Of course people can go by whatever pronoun they want.

You know your yellow Dr. Seuss books *My Book about Me*? I also loved this book when I was a child. I too filled in the blanks about myself, and answered questions like: *What do you want to be when you grow up? How many steps from your front door to the mailbox? Do you have a pet elephant?* On the very first page, the book reads: "I am a boy" or "I am a girl" with two little boxes to check one or the other. As a five-year-old, I crossed out both boxes and wrote "P-R-S-O-N." "I am a person," or prson. Spelling *person* with no *e* makes the word more vulnerable to substitution—add an *i* and you have a *prison.* I am a prison. But no matter. Somehow, I knew even at the tender age of five that checking either one of those boxes was dangerous. I don't know whether I resolutely thought that gender was a prison, or if I was just trying to be accurate in the way that writers aspire to be, when I described myself as a person.

I kept my yellow *My Book about Me* and kept adding to it as I got older. A testament to the fluidity of identity over time, several words are crossed out, rewritten, revised. At around age six, I crossed out *prson* and in pen, I checked the box: girl. I am a girl—so, ipso facto, I am no longer a person. *Person* got crossed out. I'd been schooled in the way of the world.

Eighteen years after the Dr. Seuss book, and after having written many poems, short stories, and the occasional play, I took a class in college called the Problem of Women Writing. I thought: *What's the problem? Is there a problem? A problem with women writing? A problem with women? Or with women writing?* I was compelled to take the class because it was taught by a brilliant feminist scholar. But I barely understood a word she said, so laden was her speech with words like *semiotics* and *phallogocentric.* I was desperate to learn her language. I was so intimidated by her that once, when we were next to each other at stalls in the bathroom, I could not pee and talk to her at the same time. She talked to me across the stall, and I *could not pee,* so I crumpled up some paper to make it sound like I had some other purpose and hadn't just followed her to the toilet to be near her.

On the first day of her seminar we discussed an essay by the feminist theorist Luce Irigaray called "Speculum of the Other." We spent a long time talking about her abstract, difficult argument. Finally, I, an eighteen-year-old from Illinois, raised my hand and asked innocently, "Umm—what is a speculum?" One senior yawned, and a couple of the other women looked curious. I thought it must be some philosophical term. I hadn't yet had my first gynecological exam. I was schooled that day. A speculum was no more, and no less, than a metal medical tool inserted into a woman's vagina, so that her insides can be seen by a doctor. Apparently, I was not the only woman in class who did not know.

Since that time, my daughters, I have had three children including both of you, and I have lost all shame. When you give vaginal birth to twins you become used to a roomful of people looking inside you, seeing what you cannot see. Gender when I was five years old was abstract—something that could be crossed out—I am a person, not a girl. Gender became more concrete at age six, when I put a checkmark next to the word *girl*. And then when I was eighteen, gender became abstract again—something to be analyzed, something that could be a philosophical problem. But gender when a male doctor is pulling a breech baby out of your vagina—well, that is very concrete.

Being a feminist after you have children can be more confusing. Not the title, mind you. The negotiations. By the way, I just put on three eggs to boil for breakfast. You are still asleep.

What do I wish for you, my daughters? My mother, your

grandmother, once told me that she used to pray to her Catholic God: "Please let me get one hundred on my test and be a nice person." Daughters, I hope that when you grow up you don't see any opposition between being smart and being nice. I hope there is no opposition for you between work and motherhood. Between ambition and a sense of mission. I hope if you get married that you marry men who are feminists or women who are supportive. I hope the two of you sisters are friends all your lives. I hope you find your spark. And then you find your work. I hope the world is kind to you. I hope when I get old you are nice to me. That word again: *nice*. Such an irritation for girls, Anna— your first word was a compound word—*good girl*. I hope that you are both good, but according to a strong internal compass and not always by the standards of others.

When you were even littler, there was this controversy about leaning in or leaning out. And to you I now might say— don't lean in, don't lean out, stand up straight for God's sake! You're going to need all your strength and all your posture because you will be juggling planets and plates—new weather, new politics, work, and all the rest of it. There are some lessons I learned from my grandmother that I want to pass on to you (cultivating the bonds of family, and how to cook really awful but delicious Christmas cookies), and some lessons from her that I had to unlearn, that I don't wish to pass on—stoking anger and resentment about what she gave up in order to raise five children.

Anna and Hope, you already don't ask permission to take up space. Anna, I see you in your jujitsu gi, flipping a large older boy over with your legs. I try not to get up from my seat as he then flips you over, mounts you, and chokes you until your face turns red. I hold my own breath; but there you are, flipping him over again, and breathing.

I know you both will teach me as you grow. And now I really do have to pack your lunches.

Love,

Your mama

A lesson from Hope

My youngest daughter is named Hope, and her twin brother is named William. We named them after the intersection of the streets Williams and Hope, where Tony and I met in Providence, Rhode Island. (Luckily the place names in Providence are good.) Hope is reserved, self-sufficient, self-possessed. She has always had a fairly regal bearing, even as a toddler, when she often wanted to play "coronation." She would line up her stuffed animals and dolls, then crown them. When other little girls were interested in Disney princesses, Hope was interested in *actual Queens—* Queen Victoria and Queen Elizabeth in particular. Hope's middle name is Elizabeth, after her grandmother, and she wanted a poster of Queen Elizabeth the First on her wall before she learned to read.

One day, when the twins were three, William was up all night with asthma, and I steamed the shower and held him while he coughed. The next day, bleary-eyed and fighting with the twins to put on their sneakers, I realized they needed summer shoes. It was hot and humid out, and though we hadn't yet had lunch, I rushed them to the shoe store midmorning in their double stroller. We managed to find them some sandals that fit, amid much squirming and shouting and general resistance.

Back in the double stroller, and on the way (I hoped fervently) to a nap, Hope took off her new shoes and threw them into the street.

"Naughty Hope!" I said.

Then they both started crying.

"What's wrong?" I said. "Are you hungry?"

I wheeled them into a bodega and said, "Do you want cheese? Do you want Pirate's Booty? Do you want apple juice? Do you want chocolate milk?"

The twins kept crying and throwing things out of the carriage and kicking.

"No, no, no!" they said.

"WHAT DO YOU WANT?" I said.

Then: "I want M and M'S!" screamed William.

"No, William," I said, "they don't sell M and M'S before lunch."

"I want M and M'S! I want M and M'S!"

Then I said something that I am ashamed of. I believe I said something like:

"Fine, I'll get you M and M'S if you promise to shut your face. Do you promise?"

"Yes," he said.

I gave him M&M'S, and he quieted down. But Hope continued to scream in the street, even when William started to tenderly feed her M&M'S. Her screaming was getting the better of me, and I started shouting, "Hope, what do you want? What do you want? What do you want? WHAT DO YOU WANT?" (I was like an actor's nightmare of Stanislavsky.)

Then she said softly: "I don't like you."

I had a sudden revelation.

"You don't like me because I yelled?"

"Yes!" she said, sobbing.

"Oh, Hope," I said, "I'm sorry. Will you stop crying if I am nice again? That's all you want? You want me to be my regular self?"

"Yes," she said, and stopped crying.

William promptly fell asleep, and Hope became her matter-of-fact and happy self again. I thought she wanted me to guess a thing she wanted and give that thing to her. In fact, she only wanted me to stop asking her what she wanted.

When we got home, Hope said, "Will you play with me?"

"Yes," I said. "But how about you eat something first?"

"No," she said, "play with me first, and then I will eat something."

"Okay," I said.

She began to decorate the stage, that is, a small red couch, and she said, "Here is the audience; here is the stage. Ladies and gentlemen, it's the gigu show."

"What is the gigu show?"

"I am a gate," she said. "You open me."

"Oh! Okay."

She gave me a yellow plastic key.

"How do I open you?" I asked.

"Here," she said, pointing to her heart. "Turn the key."

I tapped the yellow key on her heart, and she opened her arms, pretending that her arms were a swinging gate.

"Now walk through," she said.

I walked through the gate.

"Now you," she said.

I stood erect, frozen, a closed gate. She patted the yellow key on my heart.

And I opened my arms, swinging my arms open, a gate, and she walked through.

She was very, very pleased. And we did this over and over again.

I had underestimated the heart of my little daughter when she was crying. I thought she wanted chocolate milk. She wanted something more, and something that didn't cost any money. She wanted to open my heart; she wanted to walk in.

Learning to swim

As my children grew older, I realized that teachers-who-are-not-me could be much more helpful than I was at teaching my children many lessons. Allowing other people to teach your children is an act of faith. For example, swimming. I technically could teach my children how to swim, because I know how to swim, but I found that outside teachers were much more adept at confidently managing my children's fear of the water. While I panicked inwardly when I saw their little heads go under the water for the first time, the teacher dunked them with no hesitation.

I don't remember learning to swim, but I do remember when I jumped in a pool before I knew how to swim and my father dove in and saved my life. Perhaps that early panic made me unusually worried when my kids learned to hold their breath underwater for the first time.

When I had twins, before they could swim, I found it almost impossible to be in the water with both of them by myself. There was the ever-present danger of one slipping out of my vision or arms while holding the other one. And so I took Hope and William to group swimming classes, but I took them one at a time. Hope seemed to relish the time alone with me. As Ms. Judy taught us to blow bubbles in the water, I would hold Hope in my arms, and she would sing, "Twimmin' with Mama, twimmin' with Mama." (*Swimming* sounded like "twimming.")

And then I would pass Hope to Ms. Judy, who would dunk Hope's head underwater so that Hope could learn to hold her breath. I would likewise hold my breath as I saw her head underwater. Trusting that another person might have more expertise than you and, not only that, but that a teacher might be uniquely qualified to teach your children precisely *because they are not you*, is a lifelong process.

When my son, William, finally learned to swim, he beamed at me and said, "The water held me, Mama, it held me."

Why aren't you cheering for my sister?
Or: the headless gerbils

I sat on the sidelines when the kids were little, watching my older daughter, Anna, playing soccer, while my younger daughter, Hope, sat on my lap. The players were little and trying hard, some without support on the sidelines, so I found myself cheering for both sides occasionally.

"Good block!" I shouted as one member of the opposing team blocked the ball.

Hope looked at me fiercely, and said, "Why aren't you cheering for my sister?"

"I am!" I said.

Hope glowered. "Then why did you say *good block?*"

When the other team ultimately won, Hope said: "They won because you didn't cheer for my sister."

Oh dear, I thought. *Can we cheer for the other side and still be cheering for our sisters? When are we engaging in tribalism, and what does feminism have to do with it? And why don't sisters always cheer for one another?*

Recently I was on a conference call and I received two texts from my daughter Anna.

Mom, come home now. Come home. Come home.

Then, a call came through and I picked it up.

Anna said, "I just picked up one of the gerbils and it was only a tail. Mom—the gerbil's head is separate from its body."

Then: "Mom—I found another gerbil tail." And: "Mom—come home."

I excused myself from the conference call to go home to exhume the corpses of two gerbils.

I hadn't in fact wanted these gerbils. Nor had I wanted *four*. First Tony and the kids brought home two gerbils. The shop owner informed them that the gerbils were sisters. The kids kept thinking wistfully about the two sisters left behind. *We mustn't separate the sisters, said the children. We must take them all. Think how sad they must be.* So they went back for the other two sisters.

And then—a year later—two gerbil sisters dead, and two living. The gerbils who remained might well be murderers. Not just murderers—sororicides. One doesn't hear the term for sister-killing all that much, one hears more often of fratricide. But of my remaining gerbils, two of them ate their sisters. Whether they were dead or alive when consumed is an open question.

Why do sisters eat each other?

A sister can feel like an existential threat to another sister's well-being. The very fact of one sister's existence can send another sister into a spiral of self-doubt and murderous rage. To this day, my children deny that two gerbils murdered and ate their sisters. "It's not possible," they say, "only hamsters do that. They probably were ill, and the bodies just . . . decomposed. . . . "

But the remaining gerbils look fatter now. Their eyes look redder and beadier now. They survive, loudly eating cardboard. The sound of their nibbling is menacing, especially at night.

How to leave a meeting with a monster

I entered the Tribeca restaurant where, in his previous life, Harvey Weinstein had his special table always secured, in the back. I was early to meet him, along with a Tony Award–winning woman director who was interested in adapting one of his films into a musical with me. We came seeking permission. Something women are too often doing.

We were five minutes early and approached the hostess. It was unclear to us whether our meeting was with the Man Himself or with one of his development executives. The Man Himself was in the back at his usual table near potted palms, wildly gesticulating and shouting into his phone. The hostess at the restaurant assured us that she would bring us to his table right away. I could see him through a palm frond, and he looked angry as he harangued whoever was on the line. His most recent Broadway show had received bad reviews that morning; perhaps he was planning a war strategy to keep it running?

I told the hostess we probably shouldn't interrupt him. We could wait for his assistant to come.

"No no," the hostess insisted, "you're on the books, go on back to his table." And so we did, with some trepidation.

When we arrived at his table, he looked us over with disdain, top to bottom, and said, "Who the f*** are you?"

We gave our names. To this day I regret giving my name. The appropriate answer to "Who the f*** are you?" is "Who the f*** are you?" Not "My name is Sarah Ruhl." At any rate, we said we had a meeting with him.

"I don't know who the hell you are," he said. "Get out of here."

And so we did.

As we were walking out of the restaurant, his assistant suddenly scurried in, looking scared. She apologized for being late; a conference call had run over. Could we wait another hour to meet with the development executive?

"No, thank you," I said.

I called my agent. Did we want to reschedule the meeting? he asked.

"Reschedule it for never," I said.

I had the good fortune not to be sexually harassed by this monster, but he treated me as a thing nevertheless. Sexual predators often have failures of empathy in other departments as well.

When that producer looked me up and down and said, "Who the f*** are you?" I'd flashed on the moment when a boy in my high school turned to me and said about a fellow high school student, "She looks like she needs a good raping."

I turned red.

The boy stared at me and said, "And you just blushed."

The same feeling of dread, nausea, and disgust fell over me. The young man from my high school would, the following year, murder a pregnant woman execution-style and earn himself a life sentence. When I was sixteen, I blushed in the presence of sociopathic objectification; when I was in my forties, I walked swiftly for the door. The blush stood in for involuntary shame at another person's cruelty; the door was my salvation.

In my forties I have run into more monsters than I ever did in my twenties. That is very lucky; I have had more wherewithal to meet my monsters with my head held high. But, as a grown woman, I walked into that restaurant seeking permission from a man who didn't ask permission. In our hopes for a world with more balance and justice, women need to ask for permission less often, and men need to ask for permission. Period.

My various monsters have also taught me this: the power of art is stronger than the art of power.

Ezra the falafel maker

My favorite falafel is in Hell's Kitchen, and I go there often between rehearsals when I'm in production. I got to know Ezra, who owns the place, while eating his food. He tells customers that he makes the best falafel on the planet. I admire his confidence.

He asked me what I do, and I told him that I write plays. He asked the plot of my latest play. I told him the complicated plot, along with some of the grander themes. He just looked at me. Then he leaned forward on his elbows and said, "But where is the love story? Every good story has to have a love story."

Since then, I have always taken Ezra's advice to heart. My children complain: all your plays are about love and death.

"What else is there?" I ask them.

Not only does every play of mine have a love story, but I am also perhaps way too interested in the love stories of people I meet. If they are not currently in love, I want to know if they would like to be in love, and if I might know anyone for them. If they are currently in love, I want to know how the love came to be. I think if I had not been a playwright, I could have been a matchmaker, perhaps a deeply unsuccessful one.

When my students graduate, I tend to counsel them to make geographical decisions based on love rather than career, because the writing life is an up-and-down proposition and having someone to come home to might be more predictive of duration in the field than anything else.

The heart is smart, and the brain can be dumb. Look for the love story, said Ezra.

Lessons from critics

My first review was also my first bad review. I was twenty-four, and it was my first professional production. I remember the headline was particularly damning.

The director, Joyce Piven, also my teacher, called me the morning the review of *Orlando* came out, and said, in her unmistakable deep voice, "I'm sorry. You took the hit for me." I read the review, and saw that the critic had blamed me for a directorial decision that I had fought against. Then I took an empty glass of Smucker's jam into the basement and smashed it on the floor.

I wept, then swept up the pieces and vowed to never read reviews again.

Two years later, I was waiting in an idling car for my mother, wondering what was taking her so long in the Evanston coffee shop. As it turns out, she had spotted a friend. The friend introduced her to his date, a woman. My mother recognized the name of his date—the reviewer who had just panned my most recent play, *Melancholy Play*, in which a character gets so sad that she turns into an almond.

The woman critic and the man were on a first date after meeting online. My mother yelled, "You savaged my daughter! That's just not the function of criticism."

The critic smiled calmly at my mother. "And I do think that is the function of criticism." Critics—beware the mother. She might ruin your first date.

The great feminist Flo Kennedy once said:

> The purpose of ass-kicking is not that your ass gets kicked at the right time or for the right reason. It's that it keeps your ass sensitive.

The Buddha once said:

> Praise and blame, recognition and disregard, gain and loss, pleasure and sorrow come and go like the wind. Rest like a giant tree in the midst of them all.

*　*　*

Twenty years after my very first bad professional review, I got to break bread with the critic in Chicago. I was finally able to tell him that his review blamed me for a directorial choice I had been fighting all along. We laughed about the past; the past was redeemed.

Can we not dine with one another more often?

But what can I learn from my critics if I don't read reviews, after my vow taken over the splintered glass of a Smucker's jar?

My father once told me: "I hope you are less motivated by external opinion than your mother is."

I cannot remember why he said that, and it's not the kindest thing to have your father say about your mother. I've thought about that advice often, until it made me worry that I was depending overly on the external advice of my father. We are social creatures, after all. The meaning of our lives is affected by how we are received by others.

How is it possible to receive criticism that is genuinely given without succumbing to an overreliance on external praise or blame? A horse walks through a fire with blinders on.

Blame can be fire; praise can be fire too. All of it can be terribly distracting if the goal is to write.

Learning to receive feedback from critics begins in the writers' workshop, and when I think of developing a healthy filtration system, I turn to the blue whale as teacher. The blue whale swims and swims, and when she wants to eat, she simply opens her enormous mouth and water and garbage and krill flow in. That big blue whale has an automatic sieve system to sort out what's food and what's waste.

I think writers (and others in professions subject to almost nonstop feedback) might learn from the blue whale. We open our mouths and hear all kinds of criticism, and by the end of a formative period, we hope to have a filtration system, an automatic sieve, to retain only what feeds us. I tell my students that by the end of graduate school, I want them to be like blue whales, listening to everything but filtering out what doesn't serve them.

This can be achieved only by dedicated practice. I've seen writers listening too much to others, and their work gets pulled this way and that, until all the planks and boards have been removed and it's another ship entirely, misshapen. I've seen other writers become brittle, refusing to listen to others, becoming impervious and sealed up.

I was recently at a writers' retreat with a group of women and we made a collective list poem of all the awful things people have said to us in writers' workshops. My choicest memories of things said about my work by professors were: "I like when your main character acts like a little bitch. You should have her act like a little bitch more." And: "I find your work . . . I'm not sure how to say this"—long pause—"annoying. Do you know what I mean?"

When I need to shut out some static, I think, *Look at how the whale knows everything. Opening her mouth, swimming, moving forward, letting all that water in and out.*

One of my former students was devastated when her first professional play was panned out of town before it even came to New York, stopping the life of the play in its tracks. On her birthday, I invited her to my apartment, where my mentor, Paula Vogel, was over for dinner, serendipitously.

Paula took the former student by the shoulder, looked her in the eye, and said, "Okay. You got your cherry popped by the *New York Times*. But you got through it. You will write the next play and the next and the next."

And she did, going on to receive rave reviews in the same paper. I do not take for granted my resilience, or that of my students. Our resilience must be practiced and bolstered by our friends and our teachers.

One lesson I wish critics would learn, if they haven't already, is that their writing not only reflects reality but also creates one. To create a critical reality around a new work of art is an awesome power, and with it comes great responsibility. This critical reality, which often seems abstract, affects very concrete things, like the health insurance of actors when a play closes early.

I once heard a story from a meditation teacher who had traveled with His Holiness the Dalai Lama, and someone asked His Holiness whether a particular work of art was good or bad.

Apparently, the Dalai Lama looked perplexed, and answered: *the only measure of a work of art is how much it changes the artist.* I've tried to take that lesson to heart, and to impart it to my students. People may be busy trying to evaluate your piece of art according to external measures, or according to a set of subjective reactions that don't correspond to your intention. And you, the artist, might be so busy trying to change a paragraph, that you can't even see how the paragraph is changing you. That kind of internal change is not measurable, and often not visible. Still, we write, paint, and sing toward those invisible refinements of spirit.

Gloria Steinem

The most wonderful thing about working on a film about Gloria Steinem was getting to meet Gloria Steinem. You might think that the lessons taught by Gloria would be to do with feminism, fortitude, and fighting the good fight—and they are. And yet, when I think of her sheer presence, one of the most important qualities she has, a cousin to her eloquence, is her refined and powerful art of listening.

When I met Gloria, my health wasn't great, and it was a mystery to my doctors as to why I had cascades of bewildering symptoms. I was juggling the demands of writing and caring for three kids under the age of twelve, and I'd recently had some tough knocks from critics in the theater; the last two plays of mine had been decimated by the *New York Times*. Though I carried on writing, I was shaken.

When I first met Gloria, she was rushing from a meeting at the UN, where she was speaking about the powerful connection between countries being peaceful and equal rights for women. She was making the case to the UN that "the single most important . . . determinant of whether a country is violent within itself or . . . willing to use military violence against another country, is not poverty, not access to natural resources, not religion, or even degree of democracy, it's violence towards females."

Though Gloria had just come from an important speech to the UN, she apologized for being late to the film meeting with humility and off-handedness, as though she was late because of a subway delay. She was wearing her signature metal belt and tunic, which felt like a nod to both battle and glamour. I was starstruck. We had gathered at the apartment of the film's director, Julie Taymor, ostensibly to talk about the film, but we happened to be meeting in the early days of the Me Too movement, so there was plenty to discuss. I noticed then, as I did at every subsequent meeting, the deep quality of Gloria's listening. Listening before pronouncing, listening without interruption, listening as a vehicle for change.

Before Steinem became a household name as a feminist and writer, she had traveled to India after college. She sat in story circles in small villages with women who had experienced trauma and violence, and she was there to simply listen and hold space. Through this practice, she realized how transformative and radical the act of listening could be, and she brought the practice of listening back with her to feminist consciousness raising groups in the United States in the late sixties.

The art of listening, as practiced by Steinem, is not a performance. It's as real as can be. I've watched her quietly listen in crowded rooms where you might think she'd be holding forth, as the icon that she is. Instead, she's leaning in and listening with incredible presence to a stranger, often to a woman much younger than she.

While I worked on the screenplay for *The Glorias*, I developed a relationship with Steinem, writer to writer, rather than writer to subject. Sometimes I'd send her an essay I was working on, unrelated to the film, and she would read it quickly, which would astonish me, given her many other commitments.

Her advice to me was consistent over time—"Don't use so many quotations from other people," she'd say. "*You are the expert of your own story.*"

That was a phrase I sorely needed to hear at the time, as I was constantly going to doctor's appointments to figure out why my body was failing me; the doctors I saw often failed to recognize my own expertise. In medicine, as in so many other areas, profound listening can be transformative, even healing. Steinem argues, "One of the simplest paths to deep change is for the less powerful to speak as much as they listen, and for the more powerful to listen as much as they speak."

I learned, while researching Steinem's life, that she had a long-standing horror of public speaking and, early on in her career, would often cancel speaking engagements at the last minute. This is almost impossible to imagine after seeing her onstage, speaking with incredible fluency and charisma. I used to share Steinem's reluctance to speak in public, so I was fascinated by her arc from a writer who hated public speaking to a nonstop speaker on the road. She said she used to get so nervous when speaking in public that her mouth would go dry, like having a sweater stuck in the back of her throat. Despite her fear of public speaking, she realized that if she wanted to get her message out, she *had* to speak in public as well as write. Steinem wrote, "It was still the 1960s, and even my most open-minded editor explained that if he published an article saying women were equal, he would have to publish one next to it saying women were not—in order to be objective."

Not allowed to publish in mainstream magazines about abortion, Steinem decided to speak out about abortion instead. Steinem credits activist Dorothy Pitman Hughes with giving her the courage to speak in public; they went out on the road together and spoke to audiences as a team. When Dorothy Pitman Hughes stepped back from life on the road to care for her children, Steinem started speaking on the road with Flo Kennedy as her partner. In 1977, Bella Abzug convened the National Women's Conference in Houston. Steinem attended, later calling the conference "the most important event nobody knows about." In addition to her organizing work at the conference, Steinem had another important job—she listened. She was the unofficial notetaker for the caucuses; her listening and note-taking deepened and transformed her politics.

From ceaseless practice, Steinem ended up speaking in public as though it were her natural calling. Her life is an object lesson in resilience, the power of an unshakable mission to overcome fear, and the power of joining forces. When I asked Gloria about potential pitfalls in the film we were making about her life, she thought for a moment, and then said, "Please don't make it all about me. You need to include women who were working alongside each other at the time—Dorothy Pitman Hughes, Florynce Kennedy, Bella Abzug, Dolores Huerta, and Wilma Mankiller."

Gloria always emphasized the power of the circle—to listen to one another—and to rise together. It enraged her that she was sometimes plucked out as the face of second-wave feminism for photographs or credit, when she was joining a movement that was already underway.

She once gave me a bracelet that I treasure. I wear it when I need a boost. She had designed the bracelet herself, and it spelled out, with each bead: *We are linked, not ranked.*

Stage fright and mothers and daughters

When she was six, my daughter Anna was invited to participate in a small violin recital in our friend's apartment in our Brooklyn building. Anna waited her turn, walked to the front of the room, picked up her bow, played three notes, looked around, and froze. Then she fled the room, leaving her violin behind, and ran up two floors to our apartment, where she hid behind a chair. I ran up the stairs to follow her. Anna wouldn't speak to me, but she wrote notes, which she passed to me from behind the chair.

After an hour, she emerged, and told me that there were two kinds of stage fright: *sticky stage fright* and *liquid stage fright*. She said, "Liquid stage fright is when you feel scared before you go onstage, but once you begin to act, the fright falls off of you like liquid."

"Ah," I said. "And what about sticky stage fright?"

"Sticky stage fright," she said, "is when the fear stays on you in front of the audience and can't be rubbed out."

"And you had sticky stage fright just now?" I asked.

She nodded solemnly.

I guess sticky stage fright runs in my family. One time a theater threatened to put me on stage in my play *Eurydice* because the leading lady had vocal-rest issues and we had no understudy. I was the only one who knew the lines. I was beside myself with anxiety. Thankfully a shot of cortisol came at the right moment for our leading lady, and I did not have to go onstage.

My father often told us a story about his first piano recital, when he was playing "I Got Rhythm" at the age of seven in Davenport, Iowa. He got onstage, played the first four notes, froze, and ran out of the room. His mother made him come back and apologize to the whole auditorium. Apparently, he never played the piano after that.

Stage fright is such a bizarre phenomenon; we do something quite happily without being watched, and then, while being specifically watched, we cease to function. Before having children, my mother acted constantly in Chicago, no stage fright. After having children, she would go onstage and her heart would pound and she would feel clammy, like she was going to die. She learned later that these episodes were anxiety attacks. They kept her from the stage for a good fifteen years.

When I was twelve, we were about to go on a family trip to New York City on the train from Chicago, to see theater and take in the sights. My mother *longed* to go to New York City and devour plays. But this time, when we arrived at Union Station in Chicago, about to board, my mom started hyperventilating. She sat down and breathed into a paper bag. Her heart pounded, and she felt like she was going to die. It was quickly determined that my father would take my sister on the trip, and I would stay home with my mother, her helpmeet. I gravitated toward the caretaker role even at that tender age. My mom and I ate brownies for breakfast, popcorn for lunch, and watched movies all day. I was a little wistful for New York City, imagining my sister roller-skating in Central Park. Now that I'm about my mother's age, I wonder, more psychologically, what induced her panic attack en route to New York City. Was it that she was anxious to see the theater she probably wished she could have been acting in?

I have a photograph of my mother from her college years, looking glamorous and joyful, visiting New York City, the lights of Broadway on her face. She would have loved to have lived and acted in New York City. When she married my father and moved to Chicago from Iowa, professional theater in Chicago was just beginning, and my mother acted in that fledgling scene with great excitement, doing the work of Megan Terry and María Irene Fornés, acting in plays that protested the Vietnam War.

She continued to act when we were little, but took a solid break from acting for a decade, because of stage fright. In retrospect, I wonder if she was having hormonally induced panic attacks during menopause; she never suffered from them after her fifties. She started acting professionally again, in her seventies, never lacking for roles. No more sticky stage fright.

Sometimes mothers watch their daughters perform, but their daughters want privacy; and sometimes daughters want their mothers to perform being brave.

My daughter on dramatic irony and death

One night, when Anna was about eight, I heard her scream from the other room. It was one of those screams that makes a mother run. I dashed into the room and found her screaming over a book.

"What's wrong?" I asked.

Anna looked up breathlessly and screamed again.

"*What is it?*" I asked.

She was reading *The Little Princess* and said, "I just learned something that the character doesn't know, and now I know it, and I just want to *scream* or jump inside the book and tell the main character!"

"That's called dramatic irony," I said.

"Well, it's *awful*," Anna said, and then continued her reading.

In my life as a playwright, I tend to avoid dramatic irony. I prefer transparency in life and art rather than subtext. One could argue that death is perhaps the greatest dramatic irony of all. It's hovering all the time, and we don't see it coming. I remember when Anna was even younger, maybe four or five, and at bedtime, she asked about my father. I told her that my father had died before she was born and she said, "Where is he now?"

I said, "Heaven," hoping to be comforting.

She said, "But when is he coming back?"

"Maybe he's a baby again now," I said, hoping the idea of reincarnation might be a solace.

But she said, "I don't want to see him as a baby, I want to see him as a grown-up. I miss him!" And she commenced weeping.

She'd never met him, but I believed somehow that she missed him. I wiped away her tears and she looked up, asking, "Can dolls die?"

I said, "No, because they don't get old."

She said, "But dolls can be old, like if you have them for a long time."

I realized that she was looking for an end run around the inevitability of death.

So I said, "That's true."

"So," she said, "you can get old and not die."

I did not contradict her. She calmed down. I lay with her under the covers. And she fell asleep, head on my shoulder. I stared at the ceiling, counting the minutes when I could leave her to the mercy of her dreams, where dolls never age, dramatic irony does not exist, and no one ever dies.

When your babysitter is also your dharma teacher

When our first baby, Anna, was six months old, we kept losing our beloved artistic part-time sitters as they inevitably moved on to other jobs, like being the script prompter for Vanessa Redgrave. I looked in vain for someone to babysit while I was in rehearsals. One day, a friend called and said there was an ad in an online Brooklyn parenting forum for a sitter and it seemed of a different tone altogether than the usual. It was positively glowing, and came from a mother who, like me, wrote from home. I was ambivalent about having a full-time sitter. I didn't have one growing up, and I thought I could cobble together enough babysitting with part-time help, enough time to write a little bit here and there, or to go to auditions here and there when I had a production.

But I was about to be in rehearsals for a new play, *The Clean House*, at Lincoln Center Theater, that would involve, during previews, eight-hour days of rehearsing, watching the play in front of an audience, and then rewriting into the wee hours. I realized I was being naive about how much babysitting I needed. I had to suck it up, burn Dr. Sears's guide to attachment parenting, and admit that I needed more help. I called the number from the ad, and I made an appointment to meet with Yangzom. She walked into our apartment, and she made an instant connection with Anna. She had a grounded luminosity, kindness, and calm, and we hired her on the spot.

Yangzom's family originally came from Tibet. They were an early-refugee family to come to New York City from Nepal. Yangzom's husband did political work for the Tibetan government in exile. Yangzom had a particular gift and an easy way with babies. But as I came to observe her, she seemed to have an easy way with everyone, including me.

Yangzom and I talked a great deal when I was avoiding my writing by making tea. She told me how she carried her baby on her back through the mountains of Tibet, one week after giving birth, to get to Nepal, where she and her family would have political asylum. She told me that her brother was forced to pick flies off excrement as a child in a Chinese labor camp to show that everyone, even children, had to work. Picking flies off excrement caused a cousin in her family to go blind.

Yangzom told me all kinds of stories as we both waited for the tea to boil. At a point, I realized that she was actually giving me dharma in the form of stories. (*Dharma* is a word for Buddhist teachings.) Here is one of her stories:

A man once had four wives. His first wife loved him very much but he paid no attention to her. The second wife was younger and prettier, and he was always chasing after her, fearful she would find another man. He tried to keep her. The third wife was a very practical woman, gave the husband good advice; he relied on her. The fourth was the youngest, and he loved to pamper her.

When the man was on his deathbed, he asked, "So, which one of you will come with me to my death?" He turned to his fourth wife.

She said, "No, I will not, I will find another man after you die."

So he asked the third wife, the practical one. "Will you go with me to death?"

"No; no one can go with you to death," she said.

So he asked his second wife, the pretty one, and she said, "No, I'm busy, find someone else."

Finally, he asked his first wife, his loyal wife, and she said: "I will go with you." His wives are: fourth wife, his body; third wife, his family; second wife, his possessions. But his first wife is what you might call his soul. Only his soul can come with him after death.

I loved this story and memorized it. There is, perhaps, a certain natural reserve that comes when someone is working for your family. But when you have twins, and must work together to keep two babies healthy, much of that reserve disappears. I would often breastfeed one baby while Yangzom bottle-fed the other. She would hold William up to the nebulizer to help him breathe (his lungs weren't quite developed enough in the first few months of his life), while I would breastfeed Hope. And then we'd switch. In this switching of a baby from breast to bottle and back again, and during the long talks about Buddhism, Yangzom became family.

Yangzom knew how to make food out of seemingly nothing—a little water and flour, and poof!—there was delicious bread. If there was nothing in the cupboard but a little rice, she could concoct delicious soup. She knew how to stretch resources, make one thing into another thing, a kind of alchemy. I remember watching one time as she saved a card for a perfume ad stuck in a glossy magazine; she and her friends put on the perfume from the card when they were dressing up for a teaching with the Dalai Lama. I watched as she, her sister, and friends dressed in their traditional chupas (colorful aprons) to go hear His Holiness teach at Radio City Music Hall. Their excitement was palpable. I decided I had better buy a ticket to go see His Holiness the Dalai Lama too. I brought little Anna with me when she was a toddler, because, well, I had no babysitter—Yangzom was already there. Anna ran up and down the fancy stairs at Radio City Music Hall, and we heard the Dalai Lama dispense wisdom to his countrymen and -women in exile, and to the rest of us, who hoped to learn about compassion.

I watched Yangzom's kindnesses not only to me and my family but also to others. When her oldest friend became clinically depressed, Yangzom asked if it was okay if she brought her friend to work. I said sure. Yangzom said it wasn't good for her friend to be alone, that her friend needed to exercise and be with other people all day. I watched, as under Yangzom's watchful eye, her friend became better and better. Every weekend, I knew that Yangzom spent time helping settle other Tibetan refugees who were moving to New York City.

Before I first met Yangzom (now over a decade ago) the idea of reincarnation seemed like a distant dream, a fairy tale, to me. I was a lapsed Catholic with immense spiritual hunger. But when a former student who became a dear friend—Max Ritvo—died, it was Yangzom I asked for help. I needed a specific ritual for Max, and I wasn't going to find it in my childhood Catholic church—nor would Max have appreciated holy water from that particular dispensary. I didn't know enough about Buddhism yet to know the mourning traditions. Yangzom helped arrange for monks to come to our house to chant for Max. She taught me how to pour water into bowls, how and when to light the candles and the incense, how to pray for a good rebirth.

We came to know Yangzom's extended family, and she came to know ours. Yangzom's daughter happened to live in Chicago, as does my sister, and she helped when my sister's C-section wound was infected with MRSA, which can be fatal. My sister helped Yangzom's daughter when she had trouble with her immigration status. Yangzom was there when my mother-in-law died of pancreatic cancer in Los Angeles. We were there when her mother died of pancreatic cancer in Queens.

Yangzom's mother prayed constantly. She'd had a life of hard work and wanted to spend her last days praying and preparing for death. She had many lines on her face from being out of doors on high mountaintops with thin air, and from knowing a life of physical labor. Yangzom felt terrible that her mother was going to die in New York City, rather than Nepal, where she wanted to die.

Her mother said, "I want to die where the taste of tea is familiar."

Yangzom made her mother's last days in Queens as much like Tibet as she could manage. Monks were present when her mother died. The funeral in Astoria was packed with people. It felt like a small village. I sat next to Yangzom. When family and friends brought white cloths (or *khata*) up to cover her mother's body, it was the only time I have ever seen Yangzom cry.

In certain schools of Tibetan Buddhism, you visualize and thank the person who taught you the Tibetan alphabet in your meditation because whoever taught you the alphabet allowed you into the teachings for the first time. That could be a monk, an uncle, a mother. A teacher. Yangzom taught my children the Tibetan alphabet.

My husband's father was Thai. My father-in-law may have practiced the outer trappings of Thai Buddhism culturally, but he would not have described himself as religious. In my father-in-law's house were many Thai Buddhist relics, and he gave Tony two or three statues, which lived in our apartment. When we moved out of our apartment during a renovation, we gave Yangzom the Buddha statues so they wouldn't get harmed.

When we got back to our apartment, post-renovation, Yangzom said the Buddha statues weren't ready to come back yet. I didn't understand.

She said, "Sarah, those Buddhas were empty on the inside. You have to take them to a temple to put mantra inside, and then seal them back up again." Later that month, she brought the Buddhas back, now full of prayers, their faces painted gold.

Buddhism is a cultural inheritance for some, a philosophical position for others, and for still others, a faith that comes later in life. It somehow made all the sense in the world to me that, as a metaphor, our Buddhist practice (and statues) had been empty; for me, an insufficient Westerner's attempt. Tony had much more Buddhist context growing up than I did. When his grandfather died, he went to the funeral in Thailand. In Thailand, which practices Theravada Buddhism, mourners can become monks for a day, to grieve the dead. So Tony shaved his head, and put on monk's robes, and grieved for a man he barely knew. But for Tony, that statue of a Buddha from his father was a spiritual inheritance that did not come with any instructions. Tony's father encouraged American assimilation rather than learning about the Thai language or culture or faith.

Once, I came back from a teaching on Tibetan Buddhism with a beautiful thangka (painted scroll). And I was fixing to hang the scroll in the front hall.

"Won't it look beautiful here?" I asked Yangzom.

"No, Sarah," she said. "It would not look beautiful there. Thangkas aren't meant to be in the front hall, they are meant to be *inside*. In a prayer room. They aren't decorations."

Yangzom, as it turned out, was my teacher.

One day, I was in the kitchen making tea, and while the water was boiling, she told me a story about a distant acquaintance that astonished me. She knew of a couple, devout Buddhists from Nepal, with a restaurant in Boston. One day high lamas (monks) appeared at their restaurant and identified their son as a reincarnation of a Tibetan master. In Tibetan Buddhist tradition, when a revered teacher dies, the student looks for the reincarnation of his teacher in a child, and then becomes that child's teacher. The teacher must search far and wide for this child. And so these monks wanted to take the child, then three years old, back to the monastery in Nepal to be educated as a monk.

"What did they do?" I asked, thinking it must be an agonizing choice for a parent to make.

"They sent the child to the monastery," she said, matter-of-factly.

I kept dreaming of this story and eventually wrote a play about it, called *The Oldest Boy*.

While doing research for the play, I read book after book about Tibetan Buddhism and reincarnation. A suitcase of books! So many books! But I had no meditation teacher. Then I read a book by a teacher named Jetsunma Tenzin Palmo, one of the first Western women to do a traditional meditation for twelve years in a cave in the Himalayas. I loved her clear explanations of metaphysics, as well as the dramatic story of her life. Once, she almost got snowed in while living in a remote cave by herself; she dug herself out. A week after my fortieth birthday, I heard that Jetsunma was doing a teaching in New York City, so I decided to go. I went thinking I would just hear her speak, but at the end of the talk, she asked if anyone would like to take refuge, and I found myself raising my hand. Taking refuge in Buddhism means agreeing to five basic precepts and then having a little lock of your hair cut by a teacher.

Most of my path to that moment was inspired by the daily interactions I had with a Tibetan Buddhist who had no intention of converting me. Over the years, while observing Yangzom's preternatural calm and kindness, I decided that whatever spiritual water Yangzom was drinking, I wanted to drink too.

Jetsunma Tenzin Palmo asked me, "Are you happy for me to cut a lock of your hair?"

I said yes, and she cut a lock of my hair.

After she cut a lock of my hair, I repeated my vows, and then the Buddhist nun snapped her fingers, making it so.

Walking a dog, or a toddler

Have you ever taken a dog for a walk, particularly on a cold day, or late at night, and the dog won't do their business? And for the whole walk you think: *Pee, Pee, Pee!* And the more you inwardly scream: *Pee!*, the more the dog will not pee. There are profound moments in parenting, writing, and living in general, in which rather than simply taking the dog for a walk, you look for an outcome during the entire walk, and so you do not find it.

I remember clearly walking with my daughter Anna, then a toddler, down Fifth Avenue toward a destination that I thought would please her—a bookstore called Books of Wonder. Anna stopped every other second on the journey to point something out. She wanted to stop at every store window along the way, and she wanted to pet every passing dog. It was driving me bananas. I pulled at her hand on the busy street, rushing to get to the destination that I thought she would enjoy, instead of realizing that she was greatly enjoying the walk to the destination.

I had it all wrong. *The walk was the event.*

Why is it I seem to have to learn this lesson for myself over and over again?

As a playwright, so often the making of the thing was the thing; the rehearsal room was filled with even more delight than the production. And yet our culture values products and the personalities who make them, and not the imaginative process, which might, in the end, be the thing itself. When we hurtle toward outcome, we are rushing full throttle toward death—that's what ultimately hovers in the future.

It used to be we *had* to notice our surroundings to avoid coyotes, or quicksand. Now, as a city dweller with an iPhone, I find that it's a constant spiritual choice to take in my surroundings. We are evolving out of noticing, obsessed with destination, our phone becoming our internal compass.

And yet the very young, and the very old, remind us to be in the moment. They walk slowly and look around as they walk. When I walk with my mother (she's now eighty-two), she notices everything in her line of vision, less interested in getting where she is going, and enjoying what is along the way. I try to match her speed, try not to hurry us along.

"Look at those clouds taking up the whole horizon!" she'll exclaim, stopping to look.

"Look at those irises!"

"What is the foliage on top of that tall building?"

One day I was out of the city, writing in a little cottage. And a bird thwacked into my window. The bird thought it was flying toward the sky, but it was flying toward the glass, toward me, and it fell. In thwacking into my window, it demanded notice. I stopped what I was doing, went outside, and looked at the bird; she had a sweet little spotted chest. I realized that my window to the world killed that little bird with its illusion. And I watched the bird die on the grass.

Slow down, I thought. *Slow down and let the art-making change you.*

Giving your kids your divided attention

I think I get the most emotional information from my kids when I give them my divided attention, as opposed to my undivided attention. In Freudian psychotherapy, the patient does not look at the analyst but lies on the couch; at a confessional, a confessor does not look at the priest, who is hidden behind a curtain. Similarly, my kids tell me the most about their inner lives when I am driving them someplace. If I'm in the front seat, looking at the road and not at them, our eyes only meet in the rear-view mirror for a moment, and they tell me things. We are contained by the car, the journey is finite, and they cannot run away in the meantime. I get the least amount of information from them when I look them in the eye and ask them directly what is going on.

We hear a lot about trying to be present for our kids, but I wonder if the point is to be *almost* present, interruptible, at least by the time they can go to the bathroom by themselves. In adolescence, my kids seem to want me to be around but not talking to them; they want me in the room but not looking at them. The ideal is for me to be involved in some kind of task that is interruptible and does not require my whole focus—folding laundry, say, or cooking.

And I wonder if there is an analogue to this principle in the writing process. Paula Vogel once told me to write about grief without looking at it directly, just as you shouldn't look directly at the sun. Paula doesn't engage students directly about their trauma, conscious or unconscious. She says that to engage and transform the difficult-to-access material, the mind needs a trick, a game, a perceptual shift like standing on the head, an engagement with form so that the content can rise up and through. That's why Paula told me to write a play with a dog as a protagonist when my father had just died, rather than saying, "Write a play about the death of your father." The busy mind needed a safe container, a plaything, while wrestling with the dark undercurrents. She would give these assignments to her class: "Write a play that's impossible to stage" or "Write a play with these ingredients in forty-eight hours: a moon, time going backward, and a family secret." In other words, play a game, keep the busiest part of the mind busy so that the unruly dream life of the mind can do its magic. *Look over here, no—over there*, thinking mind.

Paula's methods tricked my mind into relaxing; they also created helpful boundaries between a student's liberty of thought and the teacher's prompts. In other words, the method utterly avoided the kind of false guru relationships that sometimes happen in graduate school, when teachers gain access to students' personal lives and also wield power. Paula has always respected the writer's privacy.

I probably have more to learn from this technique now that I am parenting teenagers. Respect their privacy. Use the power of the indirect, and the container. They are in the midst of creating their liberty of mind. I must simply drive. Ferry them around, eyes on the horizon, until they want to unburden themselves. Living in the city, I don't get as many car confessions as I would like, because I don't drive that much. Subway confessions are harder to come by.

I remember long drives with my own parents from Chicago to Iowa, where my grandparents lived. The cornfields stood at attention, quiet witnesses. The horizon line asked no questions. And we talked, and talked, and then fell into comfortable silence.

Lessons from bleeding

No one tells young girls that after you give birth, you bleed for a month. Most women learn from their own blood, and many of us don't know how to pass on those lessons, because blood has been, historically, beyond polite language.

When I was thirty-four, a year after having my first baby, I had a miscarriage. It was on Ash Wednesday, which seemed somehow appropriate for a lapsed Catholic. I walked around Brooklyn seeing ash on the foreheads of strangers and suddenly smelled the metallic odor of blood. I looked around for blood, then realized the smell was coming from my own body.

For a week, I went to bed and ate beef momos, which are Tibetan dumplings. Yangzom, our beloved babysitter, made them for me, saying I needed some iron to replace all the blood that I'd lost. I dipped momos in chutney, pretended I didn't feel devastated, and watched reruns of *30 Rock* for entertainment.

I tried to go back to my old life. But in my head was this couplet I wrote:

Every month women practice for this—
casual loss as a regular thing—
women bleed in private like animals,
men bleed in public like kings.

When I was forty-five, I landed in the ER. I had been bleeding for months, exhausted, finding myself at one point lying down on the floor in the performing arts library between the stacks, too tired to get up.

Then, while I was on a conference call about casting an opera, blood suddenly poured out of me in a new, weird, troubling way. I got off the phone quickly and walked to the nearest urgent care. The doctor took my blood pressure, blanched at the result, and sent me straight to the emergency room. They did an ultrasound and found uterine fibroids.

I had surgery to take out the fibroids, and the heavy bleeding stopped. But still, blood came and went.

For many men, and for girls before puberty, blood is the universal sign that something is wrong with the body—a sign of harm, of the body being violated, or not working correctly. A scraped knee, a bloody nose—or far worse internal and external harm. Bleeding from a place that is not supposed to bleed.

But for women, regular monthly blood is a sign that our bodies are working exactly the way they are supposed to. And so women learn to welcome blood once a month. We learn to discriminate between healthy and unhealthy blood. Does this make women fearsome to some men—that we don't fear our own blood, and instead, welcome it?

When I was forty-six, at the beginning of the pandemic, my blood stopped, seemingly altogether. For three months I seemed to be free and clear of it. The end of my reproductive life was not entirely unwelcome, as I now had three healthy children. The hot flashes began, as if on cue. I read that in Sweden and Japan women don't get hot flashes—why? Do they not drink as much red wine and coffee as we do in the States? Or was I drinking way too much red wine and coffee during a global pandemic? Probably. I tried to stop drinking, bought a ridiculous handheld fan, and took some black cohosh, an old herbal remedy that still works.

Then I promptly started bleeding again. What the hell? I bought some pregnancy tests from Walmart in case I might need them and went on with my life. Transitions are not always neat or final.

Two years later, I seemed to be done with reproductive blood altogether. On the early side, like my mother. Like clockwork, my oldest daughter started bleeding. The end of a reproductive life can be the beginning of a productive life. To me it felt something like a new virginity—exciting, blank terrain.

And I thought, *for the rest of this lifetime, my brain will be pregnant, not my body.*

Three

Flowers

What I did today:
saw the flower open in
daylight, close at night.

Anne and the natural world as teacher

I first read the work of Anne Fausto-Sterling, an eminent feminist biologist, in a gender studies class when I was eighteen. Anne wrote an important book called *Myths of Gender* in which she pulled apart pseudoscientific theories about how men and women "really are" and about how scientific investigation is itself gendered. She also happens to be married to a legendary playwright, Paula Vogel, my teacher.

When my now husband, then roommate, Tony, and I started dating, we realized suddenly that our mentors were romantically linked; his teacher was Anne, mine was Paula. They were astonished when they realized we were dating.

"Don't screw it up!" they each told us individually. They had discussed us and our work over the dining room table when we were twenty years old. Paula had read letters I'd written out loud to Anne.

Paula had always advised me to find a nice scientist. She told me it was good for artists in unstable fields (that is, the theater) to have stable partners, and she'd found one in Anne. While we were dating, Tony and I would sometimes house-sit for Paula and Anne in Providence. Anne's mid-century minimalism, her desire for her domestic life to be organized, just as her lab was, created a beautiful visual contrast with Paula's collections of Victorian teacups, theater posters, and antique Japanese fans.

Tony and I had met as housemates and reflected a similar yin-yang; Tony loves a label maker, he likes shoes in an orderly line in the entry hall, and I like to fling my coat on a chair, and I favor ancient talismans scattered around the house. Anne and Tony are scientific materialists and not big on religion or the mystical, whereas Paula and I have staked our lives on the invisible world and a theatrical profession that runs on superstition.

When we got married, Tony and I asked Anne and Paula to marry us. Tony and I did not share a specific faith (I was a lapsed Catholic about to become a Buddhist and Tony was raised by an Anglican with Thai Buddhist influences). We felt that Anne and Paula could reflect both of our belief systems. So Anne, a red-diaper baby, born to Jewish communists who eschewed religious institutions, and Paula, raised Unitarian, born to a Jewish father and Catholic mother, got ministerial certificates online from a California secular church in order to marry us. Tony felt Anne would represent his no-nonsense views on spirituality, and I felt that Paula would represent my love for the mystical in art and life. We both felt that they embodied what we hoped for in a marriage: longevity, equality, mutual respect, kindness, love, and boundaries—the hope that we would give each other liberty of mind.

A week before the wedding, Tony and I visited our wedding site, in Topanga Canyon, California, a land that the hippies never left. We wanted to buy ministerial scarves for Anne and Paula as presents. We came upon a little shop in the Topanga hills, owned by a man from Bhutan. We found red-and-gold Tibetan scarves that looked vaguely clerical and explained to the store owner that we were getting married.

"Ah, you're getting married!" he said, smiling broadly, then gave us some advice: "I wish that you love each other a lot, but not too much, not too much right away, but slowly, over time, so it doesn't explode, like a star."

So rarely does our culture give advice to young lovers about slowness. We get advice about the rightness of this or that partner, but never do we get instructions on how to love over time. I think about boiling milk, on low heat, watching all the time, so it doesn't boil over. Anne and Paula married us that November, a day that began with rain and ended with the sun coming out, and the full moon rising.

A few years later, Anne and Paula became our children's godparents, and we visited them every summer at their home on Cape Cod. While

Paula and I gossiped about the theater, Tony and Anne would walk among the flora and fauna and talk about trends in science. Anne taught our kids about biology using what they'd collected from the marsh; she made them a little aquarium on the back porch. She taught them about hermaphroditic reproduction when they found blue-eyed scallops.

Anne also taught me about plants. (I know very little about plants.) "This is sassafras," she would say, pointing. "You can tell because its three leaves are different." She has many bird feeders in her extraordinary garden and can identify birds by their calls, and she takes remarkable photographs of birds, including close-ups of hummingbirds. She taught me what quiet patience it takes to notice the natural world, and what a source of endless delight and comfort the theater of the natural world can be. Anne taught us all about the glories of swimming in ponds, and how to pick blueberries at Duck Pond, saying "It's an *echt* summer day" as she swam to the rim of the pond to grab some berries.

Anne taught the kids how to pick cucumbers from her enormous garden. She pointed out tortoise eggs laid by the side of the road. We ate dinners on the enclosed porch and watched the sunset. She would say, "There's God," pointing to the light on the water. After dinner, she taught me how to load a dishwasher to her satisfaction. I remember the first time she observed my haphazard method of loading a dishwasher, flinging dishes in this way and that, and how she raised her eyebrows. She liked to get in as many dishes as possible, in an orderly way. Tony and Anne could commiserate about loving artists who load dishwashers erratically. Anne has taught Tony over the years about the perseverance and patience it takes to love an artist—a person who burns with imaginative fervor, and sometimes looks into the middle distance instead of at their surroundings.

Usually, we visit Anne and Paula for a week at the end of summer, but the pandemic summer—when theater was shuttered—when our lives were shuttered—we spent a month there with them. We had nothing but time that summer, more time to notice the natural world. Every night, after the dishes were loaded (I got much better at the task), we would go out onto the porch and look at the stars. Anne would teach us how to look for constellations through the telescope. She taught me that the natural world was a better theater than any black box.

Every year, Anne's night-blooming cereus comes out—they bloom only once a year overnight. What an astonishment! Flowers that know how to bloom once a year! Our whole family, so used to city living, took turns putting our noses into the fragrant white petals. That night blooming cereus was teaching us to pay attention.

We breathed in a scent that was there for one night only, then we looked at the stars a little more.

On Shabbat

My father-in-law died in March 2020 of a heart attack. The pandemic made travel impossible, and so we watched his California funeral on Zoom. At one point, watching the Zoom funeral, my daughter Hope asked for popcorn.

"This is not a movie," I said. I watched the screen and felt nothing.

It was only when our friends and neighbors, the Tetzelis, came up and brought us actual food, a lasagna, that I felt the loss my husband had suffered. Through shared ritual—someone dies, you bring food—you show up—I could feel something. Shared presence, shared grief. The Tetzelis celebrated Shabbat at their apartment weekly, and often invited us. During the pandemic, this sense of community and ritual time became a lifeline, and after the pandemic was over, we often continued to celebrate Shabbat together.

We've known and adored these neighbors for the fourteen years we've lived in our building. The first night we moved in, their daughter Anya, who had heard another five-year-old girl was moving into the building, appeared at our door. Anna was already asleep, but Anya had brought her a small gift—a yellow-striped straw. Anna and Anya became best friends. Anya's mom, Mari, is a high school English teacher, and her dad, Rick, is a writer and editor, and they are always full of good talk about books and life.

Having been raised Catholic, where priests get to do all the rituals and laypeople pretty much listen, the ritual of Shabbat was, to me, a revelation. Regular people get to do the rituals! You can sing together without a priest! Regular people light the candles and bless the bread and bless the wine, in the comfort of their own homes! I suddenly thought: How did Catholicism manage to take communion away from the dining room table and away from the mothers? As I became more familiar with the songs in Hebrew, their melodies would start to stir in me on Friday mornings, my body eager for their invitation to rest in the evening.

How beautiful was my friend Mari when she approached the candles, eyes closed, and beckoned the light in with her hands. And how beautiful when her daughters were old enough to do this ritual with her. How beautiful the food and the homemade challah, and how wonderful that our friends shared these blessings with people outside their religious faith. Hearing about everyone's week around the table was a form of communion.

I once heard a climate change scientist saying that at this point in time, the most important thing you can do with the onslaught of extreme weather is to like your neighbors. You will depend on them mightily, he said, through storms, fires, and floods. The injunction to "Love your neighbor" during a pandemic or a flood becomes not at all abstract but a practical necessity, a tool of emotional and physical survival. During the pandemic, we lost so many in-person rituals. And I realized what should be obvious: that it is almost impossible to celebrate or mourn by yourself.

Abraham Joshua Heschel wrote in *The Sabbath*, "There is a realm of time where the goal is not to have but to be, not to own but to give, not to control but to share, not to subdue but to be in accord. Life goes wrong when the control of space, the acquisition of things, of space, becomes our sole concern."

Not to have but to be, not to own but to give. I'm starting to know the Shabbat songs by heart. Eventually I learned that "Shalom aleichem, malachei hashalom" means an invitation to visiting angels; a wish that they confer peace.

As a maker of theater, I am well aware of how much we need rituals to say to ourselves: now is the beginning of ritual time (in my line of work, the curtain goes up) and now is the end of ritual time (the curtain comes down, and people applaud). I didn't learn until celebrating

Shabbat with our neighbors that Shabbat has a closing ritual too, havdalah, which marks the beginning of mundane time. How wonderful to smell a handful of spices in the company of friends who feel like family.

Theater feels like family when you are in it, but it is clearly not family when you are not in it. At times, I'm sad that I moved away from the town of my birth to New York City, far from extended family. Shabbat settles this feeling of dislocation, this feeling of *How can I build a home, far from the home of my birth?* These rituals that are not my ancestors' have become an anchor for the week. And through repetition, rituals that anchor a week become an anchor for a life.

The gardener

"I'm so sorry," the gardener said again.

I'd been in Chicago for two months that summer and was still getting used to people apologizing for things that were not their fault. I was born and bred in Illinois but have lived for two decades in New York City, where people do not often apologize even for things that *are* their fault. In this case, Elizabeth, who owns a gardening shop in Evanston, Illinois, was apologizing not for something she did but for the lackluster competition. Let me explain. Post pandemic, we spent most of the summer in Evanston to be near my mom and sister.

I had been on a mission. I was buying hanging plants for my friend Mary who described herself as not having a green thumb and whose hanging plants had all died. I was staying in her painted lady Victorian house that summer, and I wanted to replace her dead plants as a favor. I don't have a green thumb either. I had the idea of buying her self-watering planters and hearty plants. I needed to find something that would be hard to kill.

First, I went to a large gardening store where they'd never heard of self-watering planters. I showed them the one planter (advertised as self-watering) that I'd bought on Amazon. The gardening store employees seemed confused and suspicious. They sold me a plant that needed bright sun. The plant withered before I could give it away.

I ventured out again to another garden shop that had been owned for four generations by the same family. As my son and I arrived, a brisk voice greeted us: "How can I help you?"

Elizabeth was a no-nonsense person, hair pulled back tightly in a bun, deep lines on her face from the sun, and she used words like *wowzers*. She immediately taught me how to use a self-watering planter. She showed me the red line in the tube indicating water level, and how the soil would wick water from the bottom. She talked confidently about plants that needed sun, plants that needed shade, plants that needed both. Then she led me over to the begonias. They were stunning. Certain flowers, when in bloom, make me believe again in God.

I complimented Elizabeth about how much more helpful and knowledgeable she was than the competition. I said, "At the last store I went to, people were not very helpful."

"Oh!" Elizabeth stopped in her tracks and said, with unmistakable sincerity, "I'm so sorry."

"Why are you sorry?" I asked, laughing. "It was the competition that was unhelpful!"

"Well, I'm sorry," she said, "because you had a bad experience. And when beginning gardeners have a bad experience, they sometimes give up." The profundity of what Elizabeth said hit me, and I looked around at all that green in the greenhouse. This was a person who cared more about the longevity of gardening than she did about crushing her rivals. She cared about the ecology of the field. I thought briefly about how the theatrical landscape in New York City could learn from Elizabeth's attitude toward gardening and the competition.

Then Elizabeth helped me pot begonias inside the hanging basket, explaining that begonias are hearty. She said "gee whiz" and expertly stuck her gloved hands in the dirt. I watched as she separated out the begonia roots and arranged them this way and that in the soil. I'd always thought there was a special mystery to planting flowers and that I was surely doing something wrong. I hadn't put my hands in soil since moving to New York City, but it looked fairly simple in Elizabeth's hands: stick your hands in the dirt with some confidence and put the roots in. I remember thinking when I was a child that grilling meat was a mysterious, difficult activity, fraught with danger, and requiring specialized knowledge, often the province of men. And once I tried grilling, I realized with astonishment that it was pretty much putting meat on a flame and flipping the meat before it burns.

Elizabeth told me to water the hanging plants every day, depending on the weather and season, but with self-watering planters, you could *maybe* get away with watering once a week. The new technology bought you just five or so days of inattention. I thanked Elizabeth profusely, and she set the new hanging baskets in the trunk of my car, telling me to water them well when I got home. She said she hadn't watered them herself because, well, sometimes that made a car dirty and that didn't go over so well with her customers. As I left, she apologized once again for the bad experience I had at her rival gardening shop.

I drove back to my temporary Victorian home and hung the baskets on the porch with my son. I was wearing the old denim gardening dress of my grandmother's that I'd recently found. It had been let out three times, mended, patched, and the pockets were enormous. The dress made me feel close to my grandmother, who was not afraid of soil.

As I stood on a ladder and hung the planters, I reflected on a few lessons from Elizabeth. First, that knowledge and warmth can be passed on to people through the exchange of objects. And that buying objects through the internet might get you new objects quickly, but it won't get you oral tradition.

Elizabeth also taught me that some people actually love what they do more than they love outselling the competition. And that plants really do require attention, and water. I watered Mary's plants and thought about my roots, deep in Illinois and Iowa, and how long it's been since I've watered them.

My dog knows everything

Are there really that many differences between me and my dog? She eats from a bowl on the floor. I eat from a bowl on the table. She bears small irritations with grace; I *sometimes* bear small irritations with grace. Like many dog owners, I aspire to be more like my dog. My family jokes that my dog Minerva, a small white Havanese, can't stand to be even two feet away from me; she's like my daemon from *The Golden Compass*.

I go to a party with my dog, saying, "I have brought my dog with me."

"Why?" asks the host.

I answer, "Because everything in life is better with a dog. Except for sex."

I believe that dogs know everything: love, hunger, grief; how to wait for the beloved to come home. Recently I had to be away from Minerva for a month while I worked in England. I missed her so much that I once tried to text her. That is to say, I started to text the dog sitter, *How is Minerva doing?* But I realized I was typing M-I-N-E-R-V-A as my contact. If only Minerva could text me back!

Minerva is not afraid of death. But she knows the smell of death will protect her from predators. So when she gets the chance, she rubs herself in the carcasses of dead animals: birds and fish. I do not want to rub myself in the carcasses of dead animals. How do I protect myself from death? By rubbing myself with words?

Dogs truly understand friendship. If a dog loves another dog, and if that dog friend gets the hiccups, they'll lick their friend's eyeballs until the hiccups go away. Friendship between dogs is profound and embodied. How can I make my friend's hiccups go away? I don't lick their eyeballs. How can I help a friend's sadness go away? Is there an embodied way to show my care without licking their eyeballs?

Dogs know how to live utterly and completely in the moment. Unless they smell a whiff that brings them into the past. Sometimes Minerva tries to walk back into the past, as if the past were a smell, like a house no longer inhabited. Or the scent of an old friend's urine. For a dog, the past is present only in the nose—oh, holy nose! At a familiar smell, how Minerva strains against the leash. How we all strain against the leash of time.

A dog will poop on any lawn, a beautiful or an ugly one. Just as the moon rises as surely over an ugly house as a pretty one. People are always making distinctions between ugly and pretty lawns, ugly and pretty people, whereas for the dog mind, what matters is love, death, exits, and entrances. Sometimes I think Minerva does my writing for me while she dreams. I wake, take dictation, and drink tea.

Max, or learning from your student

I first met the poet Max Ritvo when he was a Yale senior in my playwriting workshop. In his application to get into my playwriting class, he wrote, "All I want to do is write." He had a luminous quicksilver mind, an open heart, a wild sense of humor, and a rare and unmistakable poetic gift. That fall, he also had a recurrence of Ewing's sarcoma, a pediatric cancer. He worked hard to graduate from college while undergoing chemotherapy, writing poetry all the while.

After his graduation, we wrote long letters in the form of email back and forth. Over the next three years, we became close friends and literary confidants; we discussed everything from poetry to pop music to child-rearing to our enduring love of soup.

Max and I continued to write to each other while he went on experimental trials. When he moved to New York City to get his MFA at Columbia, we met in person for meals, and argued about John Berryman, the meaning of *Madame Bovary*, deconstructionism, and whether or not there was an afterlife. Max thought there was no afterlife. I thought there was, or at the very least, I thought the soul was immortal. (Whether or not there is a soul and whether or not it is immortal is a sticky and not-agreed-upon issue in Buddhism, but I decided to gamble on the soul.) Max could slide into discussions of spiritual matters as easily as most people talk about the weather. When I took refuge in Tibetan Buddhism, I told Max all about it, and he said, "I'm so happy you took refuge with an awesome Himalaya-trekking nun."

Unlike me, Max was an extroverted writer. When he read his poems aloud, he shouted them to a crowded room, circling and often wearing a pink kimono. He collected friends readily, demonstratively, across geographical barriers. Max knew he didn't have time for the slow reveal. He once recited a poem he'd written, standing up, with his booming voice in a small Brooklyn café while I faced him.

When I indicated a measure of embarrassment, Max was horrified and apologetic, waving his arms.

"I embarrassed you!" he said.

"No, no," I assured him. "I'm embarrassed in exactly the right way, like Elizabeth Bishop when she read a poem that moved her."

"Bullshit!" Max said.

Martin Buber wrote about the moment that the teacher/student relationship turns into friendship.

> However intense the mutuality of giving and taking with which [the teacher] is bound to the pupil ... [t]he teacher experiences the pupil's being educated but the pupil cannot experience the educating of the educator. .... In the moment when the pupil is able to throw himself across and experience from over there, the educative relation would be burst asunder, or change into friendship. We call friendship the third form of the dialogical relation. .... It is the true inclusion of one another by human souls.

In other words, Buber argues that the student should not, or cannot, experience what the teacher is experiencing, but when the student's empathy is wide and wise enough, the student crosses over, and the relationship is transformed into a friendship.

Without my noticing, Max became my teacher.

Max pretty much jumped over that bridge with all of his teachers, as far as I know—Louise Glück, for one, and Lucie Brock-Broido. He could not be content with only being on the receiving end.

Max encouraged me to publish my poems for the first time, and to read them aloud. Having started as a poet, moving into playwriting in my early twenties, I still wrote and squirreled poems away in my desk. Max asked me to share these poems with him, and it was well-nigh impossible to say no to him, so I let him read them. Then he asked me to read my poems out loud with him in front of audiences, which had always made me feel a vulnerability akin to vertigo, but for Max, I did.

When Max was at the National Institutes of Health in Washington, DC, undergoing clinical trials, we wrote letters, swapping poems, plays, rants, jokes, spiritual questions. At some point we decided to make a little book of these letters. We wrote on subjects as far afield as metaphysics, literary revenge, meditation, the Amtrak quiet car, our mutual love of Mel Brooks, and the nature of friendship. We arranged and rearranged our book while Max was alive, and argued about structure. To organize it chronologically was to imply an ending, which neither of us wanted.

The ending came that August, when he was twenty-five. A lot of people pointed out that Max was the same age as Keats when he died. I don't even know if Max liked Keats, though I would still love to ask him.

After Max died, I dreamed of him frequently. In one dream, I asked him if it was hard to be dead. He said: *Yes, it's hard to be dead. It's hard not to talk. But I am listening all the time.*

My husband had warned me about the torrent of grief I would have after Max died.

"I'm his teacher," I told my husband, as if that role protected me from grief. As though teachers are not human, as though they're inured from loss.

Max left behind a mother, father, and sisters in mourning, as well as a young widow, literary admirers, legions of friends, and several teachers who he flipped from teachers into students. He also left behind his first book of poetry, *Four Reincarnations*, which Milkweed Editions had rushed to press so Max could hold the galleys in his hands. Surely, he is the only poet to have had his debut collection vie with the *Odyssey* for best-selling poetry book on Amazon on the day it came out, shortly after his death.

I poured my grief for Max into finishing our book, *Letters from Max*. I never thought the book could be a play, my usual form, because it seemed too personal, too quiet; also, it seemed taboo to have an actor *play* Max, or, God forbid, for an actor to play me. But the more I did public readings of the book, I saw that the book was naturally in dialogue form, and seemed to cry out for human voices to embody it. So I did make the book into a play and was ultimately moved to see young actors connecting deeply with Max's language, vaulting him back into the present moment, embodied.

What are the rituals for the loss of a student, or a teacher? We are not family; we do not say goodbye at the bedside. And yet the ability of a teacher or student to transform one another's lives can be epic. Sometimes we have to create our own rituals of remembrance; in my case, it was a play.

Max was the voice that answered back. He still is. Max taught me not to wait for the slow reveal, to tell people you love them now and often. And he taught me that students sometimes make the best teachers.

Lesson on an Amtrak train from a monk

When Lincoln Center Theater produced my play *The Oldest Boy*, we had Tibetan monks come in to speak with the cast. As part of our research, a monk named Khenpo Pema Wangdak visited us to speak about his understanding of reincarnation. At one point he said, laughing, "Art and religion aren't very different. And someone's got to do it."

I learned that Khenpo Pema Wangdak escaped Tibet after the Chinese invasion in 1959, and that he was the only child of five to have survived the escape. Despite his tragic childhood, I was struck by the optimism and equanimity written on his face, which was also very thin, lit up with brown eyes, and wreathed in smile lines. I learned that he'd created a Tibetan system of braille, and though he was a very distinguished teacher with many honors, he carried himself with the utmost humility and simplicity. His head was shaved clean, and his hands were graceful. He spoke to us with good humor, and fluid eloquence, about the experience of being trained as a monk from a young age.

Months later, I was in Penn Station waiting for a train to New Haven, which I did on a weekly basis to teach at Yale. I was reading *The Asian Journal of Thomas Merton*. I've always loved Merton the mystic, rebel, and poet. I also love his ecumenical openness to Zen and Tibetan Buddhism, though he was a Catholic Trappist monk.

As I read about Merton being offered advice by a Tibetan lama to find a teacher, I decided to get up and buy some water for my journey. Upon getting up, I saw a monk in maroon robes standing quite naturally by a column, in the midst of the chaos of Penn Station, reading a book. I recognized the very same Lama Pema who had advised me on my play.

"Hello," I said.

He smiled and said hello, not at all surprised to see me.

"What are you reading?" I asked him.

"An autobiography of His Holiness the Dalai Lama," he said, "that I've read at least one hundred times. What are you reading?" he asked.

"Thomas Merton," I said, "about his travels to Asia."

"Ah yes," he said, looking at my book. "Here, you will see the hand-writing of my teacher," and he pointed to the page in the book where I had stopped reading.

"*What?*" I asked, in disbelief.

On that very page, Merton had published a handwritten note from a Tibetan lama, the teacher of the very same teacher standing next to me. That I was reading the handwriting of his former teacher did not seem extraordinary to Lama Pema, but I was stunned.

I bought water for both of us, then we sat on the train together for two hours and he talked. He held my gaze with such presence and steadiness. I don't know if he noticed the facial paralysis I'd had at that point for years, but he said to me, "It is possible to smile. It is always possible."

I had searched long and hard for Buddhist teachings from books, and then suddenly a teacher was staring me in the face at a train station, not to be ignored. A teacher had appeared! After that train ride with Lama Pema, I went to one of his teachings in New York City and listened to his instructions on meditation and the practice of compassion. I visited his simple apartment where he taught. As we spoke, he made himself a bowl of oatmeal, one of his two meals a day, I think. His apartment was full of butter lamps and scrolls.

A year after my former student Max died, I went to Lama Pema's apartment so that he could do a ritual; in Tibetan Buddhism, you chant for the dead on the one-year anniversary. We called in Max's mother from California so she could listen.

After the chanting, Lama Pema said to us, "It is very sad to die so young, to die so early. On the other hand, when you wake up from a dream, it doesn't matter how long the dream was. You never remember how long the dream was. The important thing is that you wake up."

When your shrink is also your dharma teacher

I found Dr. M when I was in dire straits. I had facial paralysis from Bell's Palsy that would simply not go away. The inability to smile had become both metaphor and reality; an internal and external state. I was full of self-loathing; I blamed myself for all of my exhaustion and for my perceived failures as a mother to three small children. I also felt like a lackluster wife and partner and thought maybe my family would do better with a more energetic, cheerful replacement of me.

I did not believe all of my thoughts fully, thank God. But the hopeless, ashamed feelings kept intruding, unbidden. A friend gave me Dr. M's number. Dr. M is a well-known writer, Buddhist practitioner, and psychiatrist. (It's probably silly of me to call him Dr. M because you could probably google him easily and find out who he is by looking at the acknowledgments of this book, but I sort of enjoy the literary pretense of calling him Dr. M; it makes me feel mysterious.)

Dr. M is compassionate, and an incredible listener. He bobs his head back and forth, listening. He is also funny, which is good medicine for me. Rather than excavate my pain and dwell on it, or dig around for childhood traumas, Dr. M kept me in the moment. He seemed always to be more interested in my health and my natural abilities than he was interested in my despair. When I felt good, he wanted to keep me that way rather than looking for more hidden neuroses. He taught me to leave unwelcome emotions alone; to nod to them and then leave them on my plate like unfinished vegetables. At first I did not understand this method. The only kind of therapy I'd had in the past poked around at an emotion until it seemed to get worse. "Leave it alone," Dr. M would say. Under his care, I got better.

The other day I was talking to Dr. M and I was describing a Buddhist

I knew who seemed to get angrier and angrier the more they meditated. We were talking about spiritual attainment and if anyone ever *really* gets better, and he said he remembered being at a Buddhism and psychotherapy conference years ago where someone said, "What do Buddhism and psychoanalysis have in common? Neither one of them work!"

Then we both laughed. There was a pause. And then I said, more seriously, "So, if nothing really works in the end, what is the goal?"

"Lightness," he said. "Lightness."

The healing power of literature

I am doubled over with a large needle in my spine. I tell the neurologist inserting the needle that I'm about to pass out. I'm getting a spinal tap to see if Lyme disease has made its way into my cerebral spinal fluid, and therefore into my central nervous system. The doctor tells me, with great compassion, that she needs to finish the spinal tap to see what's going on inside my body. I tell them I can stand the pain (just barely), but that I might pass out or throw up. A medical resident runs to get a vial of ammonia and puts it under my nose. I breathe in ammonia, and suddenly, magically, I'm no longer faint. The pain is very present, but the nausea is gone and I feel like a real nineteenth-century lady, revived with smelling salts.

Thirteen years of wondering what's wrong with me has finally landed me here at Stony Brook hospital with a needle in my spine. The left side of my face was paralyzed after I gave birth to my twins. The neurologist diagnosed Bell's palsy, which is the paralysis of the seventh cranial nerve. No one knows exactly how you get it, or how, and if, it will heal, though it can be associated with pregnancy, viruses, and Lyme disease. For the vast majority of patients, the facial paralysis goes away completely in three months. In my case, it stayed. And stayed. And stayed.

And so, ten years after diagnosis, I hunkered down to write a book about the loss of a smile, the hope for a smile, and the acceptance of a new face. Writing the book helped me make sense of my own story, which was itself healing. The writing process put my illness, quite literally, in the past tense, even though my biological healing was still incomplete.

After *Smile*'s publication, I received all kinds of letters and messages from readers who identified with my story. One woman wrote that she got Bell's palsy after giving birth; she said the psychological pain of Bell's was far worse than labor pain. Another woman wrote that she'd been an actress but stopped acting altogether after her face developed asymmetry.

Then, out of the blue, a retired infectious disease doctor who read an excerpt of the book got in touch with me. Over the phone, he diagnosed me with late-stage neurological Lyme disease. I was shocked. I told him that three months after the onset of Bell's palsy, I had blood tests for Lyme that were negative, but this doctor told me that certain kinds of Lyme can go undetected in basic blood work, and that there are many false negatives—in fact, 30 percent.

I flashed on a memory. When I was three months pregnant with the twins, Tony and Anna and I had gone for the weekend to a cabin in Long Island, owned by friends. They had said generously, "Come stay at our shack in the woods and relax!" And I thought—that must be a euphemism, because I'd seen their well-appointed apartment at the Dakota. We arrived, and it was, in fact, a shack in the woods. Within a day of being there, Tony got a tick bite and a classic rash—a bull's-eye—on his leg. He sent a photo of the rash to his doctor and took antibiotics right away. I never had a rash or a tick bite that I could see, so I tucked the incident away in the back of my mind for years.

I'd certainly had many of the symptoms, a litany actually, one after the other. I'd gotten used to seeing specialists every three or four months as new strange symptoms cropped up and, sometimes, disappeared. Lyme is called the "great imitator" and is hard to diagnose because it affects so many systems and shifts course constantly. As soon as my headaches stopped, I would be on my way to an ophthalmologist with new strange ocular symptoms. The march of the symptoms included facial palsy, migraines, benign tremors, tics, strange eye pain, postpartum depression, peripheral neuropathy, and crushing fatigue. Over the past thirteen years, I had become so used to being tired that I thought it was normal. I rarely stayed up past the children's bedtimes; I napped whenever I could in the afternoon, woke late in the morning in a fog, and was horrified at the thought of any strenuous exercise. If I drove for more than an hour at a time, I would start falling asleep at the wheel. I could explain away the fatigue—I had three young children and a busy career. But even as the children started sleeping through the night, and I did too, the exhaustion stayed with me. I felt often like a piece of dried-out, day-old toast.

My body's breakdown eventually included extreme digestive troubles, which I thought could be explained by my having celiac disease, recently diagnosed. Maybe I had eaten gluten? Or had food poisoning? But that weird pepperoni was months ago, and the diarrhea persisted night and day. I lost twenty pounds. I shat myself on the train on the way to teach. There was clearly something very wrong with me. My husband did more and more caretaking of me and the kids, giving up hobbies like martial arts so he could handle mornings while I slept or sat on the toilet. I saw more and more specialists. I finally landed in the hospital with a colonoscopy. When I'd looked up at the gastroenterologist after the scope, still on truth-serum anesthesia, I said what first came to mind, thinking of my father, "Do I have cancer?"

"No," she said, and I thought, oddly, that I detected a smile on her face.

"But you do have these." And she showed me a jar in which tiny but visible worms were swimming. My eyes widened.

"I vacuumed these out of your colon," she said. "You have parasites. You'll need antibiotics. But you're fine."

I had no idea where I'd gotten the parasites, nor did I have any idea that Lyme makes you more susceptible to getting them. I took antibiotics, got rid of the worms, and went on with my life. But more strange symptoms surfaced: burning in the ear, lack of balance, bumping into walls.

After the infectious disease doctor called me out of the blue, telling me over the phone that I had Lyme disease, I started to investigate. At first

I was incredulous, how could I possibly have Lyme if I'd seen dozens of specialists over the years who had never caught it? Doctor after New York City doctor had seen me as another mysteriously chronically ill patient and shrugged or given me a questionnaire about "stress." When I tried to get more specific Lyme blood work done, one infectious disease doctor even yelled at me; little did I know that Lyme is a political and medical third rail, and that New York City doctors are probably the least equipped to diagnose it because city doctors see the disease less often. It was no accident that I finally had to leave the city and see a specialist in Long Island, where Lyme is endemic, to get an actual diagnosis and treatment.

The neurologist I saw at Stony Brook hospital after thirteen years of troubles asked me why I'd never had a spinal tap. She said, "You have symptoms in almost every system in your body, you and your husband were clearly exposed to Lyme in Long Island when you visited before onset of your symptoms, and you have unrecovered Bell's palsy, for which Lyme is a differential diagnosis."

"I don't know why I've never had a spinal tap," I said. "I guess I never saw the right doctor."

She ordered a spinal tap, and a new set of more extensive blood work, looking for specific Lyme antibodies. The results were strongly positive. As was the spinal tap. I felt bewildered, angry, and full of grief for all the lost time—time spent sleeping, time spent chasing specialists, time spent not being believed by medical professionals. I wanted to know how thirteen years of specialists had missed a crucial diagnosis, had looked only at blood work rather than seeing the whole patient, had looked at numbers rather than story.

The Stony Brook neurologist warned me that my facial nerve was probably too damaged at this point to improve with treatment, but that it was important to treat the Lyme to prevent future adverse neurological effects. I think her exact words were "You'll probably never feel like your old self again, but maybe you'll feel a little better. The main thing is to do the treatment and get on with your life."

So I went on IV antibiotics for a month. I was given a port in my arm, and a wonderful nurse came to teach me how to inject myself daily and how to flush out my port with saline. I was in rehearsals for a new play at the time, and I would inject myself daily before going to the theater. The play was emotional, as was the treatment. At one point the back of my head swelled up, I was worried I had some kind of lump; Tony said no, it's your lymph nodes clearing out the infection.

I started to speak to other people in my theater community who had been through Lyme. I learned from them which doctors to seek, which ones to avoid. I learned how many others had been disbelieved by doctors who didn't believe neurological Lyme was a thing, like my own internal medicine doctor. I learned how important community is when you have a chronic illness. I learned that once people are done with treatment, sometimes they want nothing to do with the Lyme community, or with spreading awareness, because the process of getting a diagnosis can be such a nightmare, along with the symptoms, and patients just want to be done with it and move on. One little tick. One little goddam tick. How could such a small thing wreak such havoc?

After a month of IV antibiotics, slowly but surely, I started to feel as though I had more physical energy again. Now, a year posttreatment, I'm walking more, writing more, and sleeping less. I have fewer doctor's appointments. I wake up in the morning and can function before I have caffeine. I have a greater sensation of well-being. I feel a little bit like Rip Van Winkle, awakened after a long sleep. People sometimes ask me how I was able to be productive when I was ill for so long. I think that I continued to write because I had to—writing was a form of prayer. The less physical energy I had, the more mental energy I tried to produce in order to compensate, and to feel alive. Now, life has more balance. More cooking and reading. More walking and writing.

This morning, I woke up before everyone else in the household, showered, and made breakfast. Then I went back to bed and into my husband's arms.

"You're up early," he said.

And then he said, "I've missed you."

"What do you mean?" I asked.

He said, "I missed you when you were sick."

I have immense gratitude for that reader who finally helped me get a diagnosis. I learned that readers can, quite literally, be healers, and that writing a book can save your life.

The show must not go on

From time immemorial our mantra in show business was: *The show must go on.* You're sick? *Get into your costume.* You're scared? *Get onstage.*

The brilliant actress Kathy Chalfant was once wounded by a sword fight in my play *For Peter Pan on Her 70th Birthday*, and her flesh was literally dangling from her arm, and she was bleeding while flying. *The show must go on!* She didn't miss a beat onstage, dueling with Captain Hook and contemplating mortality while bleeding. She went to the emergency room after the show and got stitched up, accompanied by the actor playing Captain Hook. Captain Hook was a wreck, felt responsible for wounding his dear friend. That was back in the pre-pandemic land of *the show must go on.*

You have a high fever or feel like throwing up? The show must go on. Your grandmother died in the Midwest and you want to go to the funeral? No, the show must go on. This is how show people have existed for hundreds of years.

And then came Covid. And we learned that sometimes: the show must not go on.

This reversal was wild and hard to metabolize. Two years of the show not going on at all; two years of: the show *must not* go on. Around the world, actors fled their dressing rooms and went home. Two years of quiet, isolation, patience, despair. Then we came back to the theater frightened, canceling a whole show because an actor had a cough. Three hundred seats of lost revenue for a sneeze, unheard of in the old days. In many ways, the new rules signal a more compassionate way to make theater. They allow for the reality that life happens—that people get sick, babies get born, parents die, and you simply cannot go on.

Still, show people have to believe that theater is very important in order to do their jobs. We are communally assenting to a reality that is imaginary and, in order to pull off that magic trick, we have to think that the unreal is very important. So important that we would not go to a funeral, or tend to a sick child, because this alternate reality demands our participation.

Theater folk exist in a state of a perpetual emergency. And yet, it's almost never *really* an emergency. It *feels* like an emergency in that people are coming to watch you imminently, and you must be ready. But it's almost never really an emergency in that it's make-believe. In order to maintain a state of artistic fervor, real bodily emergencies are often ignored in the theater.

I remember one actor I worked with who had been sobbing, in a state of heightened catharsis, after a rehearsal and he blew his nose hard, and out came a lot of blood and a strange bloody organic-seeming object, the size of a dime. So he called me for advice, and sent me a photo of the mystery blob because my husband is a doctor and he thought we could assess whether he needed to see a specialist. The bloody discharge was indeed odd, like an alien life-form, or a bit of coral. The actor was worried he might have blown out a bit of cartilage, or brain, into the tissue; or was it a cosmic blob expelled by catharsis? I sent the photo to an ENT doctor friend who couldn't figure out what the hell it was; the doctor said the actor should come in person to be assessed.

It turned out the bloody discharge was a bit of sponge; the actor had been a guest on a television show where he needed to be in a fight scene months ago, and the blood-soaked sponge stuck up his nose for the fight scene had never been properly removed by the makeup artist. The mystery was solved. And I was reminded of how we fake bodily emergencies onstage, while ignoring the possibility of real ones.

But now, all bets are off. The show only *might* go on.

Recently, an hour before the opening of my play *Orlando*, the stage manager called the director to the theater for an emergency. The director rushed over.

"What happened?" he asked. The stage manager explained that an actor, I'll call them J, had eaten a cookie in the green room that tasted weird, and a little plantlike. So they asked the actor who had baked the festive opening-night treat, we'll call her L, "Is there any weed in the cookies?" L heard the word *wheat* for the word *weed* and said, "Yes." As in, yes, there was wheat in the cookies; but J assumed the "yes" meant there was *weed* in the cookies. J panicked. Their body reacted badly to marijuana, and J felt that it might be impossible to go onstage while high. The word spread throughout the cast like wildfire that there was weed in the cookies.

The star of the show said, "Oh dear, I had five. We'll see what happens."

As the director was being updated on the situation, L came running down the hall crying out, "Wheat! Wheat! There's *wheat* in the cookies! I wouldn't even know where to buy pot!"

And so all the actors calmed down and went onstage. I love this story because I find it hilarious, and also because the show actually went on, no harm done.

Now, if the performers had actually been accidentally high, would they have had to go onstage in this post-pandemic world? The rules have changed. We no longer have to muscle through extreme discomfort in quite the same way in the theater. And this transformation is not particular to the theater post-pandemic. So many events, rituals, and practices that seemed *essential* pre-pandemic turn out now to be optional. Going into the office? Eh. Going to that destination wedding? Meh. An essential-seeming party when under the weather? No. The need to perform that we're all right when we are *not* all right is becoming less essential.

What might this new world look like, a world in which we do not have to perform when we are not well? In how many professions are we softening the edges? Perhaps, after a global pandemic, we are learning to acknowledge real emergencies. Perhaps we have opened up an avenue for grace inside our mania for productivity. And yet . . . there are times back in the theater where I feel more fear, more rush, than ever before. We are out of practice.

Inside the shuttered dressing rooms during the pandemic were tiny museums, interrupted altars to presence. Actors had to leave their things exactly as they were and exit the building, for over a year. I think of those little abandoned talismans—opening-night cards, lipstick, flowers, lucky charms, under mirrors surrounded with light bulbs. We are coming back to presence now, and allowing for the reality of lived emergencies inside the fictional worlds we are building. I can only hope that we are coming back kinder.

Learning from Scheherazade
while binge-watching Succession

Once upon a time, a long time ago, two royal brothers found their wives humping the help. So the two princelings decided that all women were evil. One brother decided that he should marry again, because ecstatic love helps men reach God; but because he did not trust women, he decided to marry a new woman every day and have her slaughtered the following morning.

Droves of daughters in the kingdom were slaughtered after being bride-for-a-day. One wise woman, Scheherazade, a philosopher-poet-storyteller—decided to marry the shah in order to save the other women in the kingdom. She told stories to the king without end—she created such desire in the king for plot—*What would happen next?*—that he would spare her every morning. He wanted to know what happened more than he wanted to kill his bride.

Story followed story—and Scheherazade kept spinning her tales with lessons embedded in them—mostly lessons about the evil that men do. Time passed, with the king's erotic desire for story always burning, never quite finished, and in the meantime, Scheherazade had one child, then two, telling a story every night to keep from being killed. Tales of magic carpets, Ali Baba, Aladdin . . . When she reached a thousand and one nights of tales, she asked for the gift of life so that she could raise their sons. The shah admitted that he'd fallen in love with her through her tales, and he allowed her to live.

While I first had Covid and binge-watched *Succession*, I thought about Scheherazade and wondered—is there a violence to plot? To cliff-hangers? To the tantalizing question of what will come next? I felt so sick, but knowing I could watch an unfolding story day after day made me feel a little bit more alive.

I had never written for television, but I now had such gratitude for the television writers who wrote for their lives—charged with creating endless appetite in the audience for receiving yet another story—or else being fired. Just like Scheherazade, they had to feed the belly of the beast—the desire for plot—or else be erased.

After ten days of Covid I'd watched two seasons of *Succession*, watching at the rate of about two episodes per day. Afterward, I felt as if I'd binged on food—bloated and a little bit morally bankrupt.

The ongoing series form in general has always given me a bit of terror because it creates appetite without catharsis. Good television forestalls satisfaction, creates desire for more and more plot without ever satisfying it—in order to create more watching. Soap operas are designed *never to end*. A beginning with an endless middle feels to me like a mythical creature—all stomach, no heart. When I was seventeen, I wrote a pretentious story called "The Absence of Plot." I wondered what a short story without a plot would be. I should have realized that others, like Gertrude Stein, had already figured that out.

Binge-watching while having Covid somehow made me associate illness with television. And the endless void-filling as form began to strike terror into my heart. Scheherazade had to keep spinning tales until her boys were old enough that the king would love them; many television writers have to spin tales for at least seven seasons so that the episodes will go into syndication, a kind of immortality.

The craving for more and more plot without catharsis feels linked somehow to our culture's desire for sex without love, for violence without emotion. From time immemorial, did writers try to prevent actual violence by creating fictional violence? Or are we just desperately in denial about our own hungers?

I recovered from Covid. Three times. And *Succession* ended after four seasons with an amazing catharsis. I sometimes think people are scared of chronic illnesses because there is no arc, no catharsis. The damn thing just goes on and on, like bad television. Imagine Dickens or George Eliot writing those long novels in serialized form but *never finishing them.* One might argue that if you can at least *imagine* an ending, you have the possibility of lasting art. Or if you can *imagine* the possibility of healing, you can get yourself out of the slough of despond.

And yet . . . and yet . . . sometimes we are just in the midst of story. Or illness. No bird's-eye view. Just an unfolding. Like Scheherazade, making up story after story in order to stay alive.

Penelope, weaving and revising

Penelope, that faithful wife in the *Odyssey*, wove and unwove the same tapestry, waiting for Odysseus to come home. She didn't want to finish that tapestry; she wanted to deceive her suitors. "So by day she'd weave at her great and growing web—by night, by the light of torches set beside her, she would unravel all she'd done. Three whole years she deceived us blind, seduced us with this scheme." Penelope was smart not to finish her tapestry, for when it was done, she would have to consider unwanted marriage proposals. Like Scheherazade, her continual storytelling protected her bodily integrity.

I learned about the *Odyssey* from my mother, who taught it to first-year girls every year at Regina Dominican high school, and from Jane Schwalbach, my own freshman high school English teacher. My mother was obsessed with the *Odyssey*. The head nun at her school, my mother's boss, would complain that my mother taught the book too slowly. But my mother loved to savor it with her students, going through the text bit by bit, unpacking imagery. The head nun thought that what made for excellent teachers was getting through the material efficiently. My mother, like Penelope, savored the process, and went around the house quoting Homeric epithets.

Jane Schwalbach would read out couplets from the *Odyssey* to us in her rich sonorous voice, walking around the room in her clackety heels and proclaiming her favorite mantra, "Through suffering comes growth!" She wanted us to know that Odysseus grew up through his odyssey, that he was transformed by his challenges. I suppose that is important for a fourteen-year-old to know.

Now, all grown up, when I think of the *Odyssey*, what stays with me is less the hero's travails and more Penelope as a figure for the artist, in a perpetual process. Penelope had a peculiar method to her madness; she weaved and unweaved and was rewarded for her labors. Whereas the artist who rests in perpetual process without ever finishing is never rewarded for that labor, is never done, and the artist becomes a victim of their own perseverating.

I think of a poem, "North Haven," written by Elizabeth Bishop for her dear friend Robert Lowell after he died. Bishop writes, "Nature repeats herself, or almost does: / repeat, repeat, repeat; revise, revise, revise." Lowell was an obsessive rewriter, both a blessing and a curse. When he was sane, his proclivity for revision was probably very helpful; but when he was in the hospital for mania, as he was with regularity, his rewriting became a kind of madness. At the psychiatric hospital, he would take a whole book of his poems and rewrite them all as sonnets in a week. Weaving and unweaving. In "North Haven," Bishop equates the inability to revise with not being alive. She writes, "You can't derange, or rearrange / your poems again . . . sad friend, you cannot change." As beautiful as I find this sentiment—that life is inevitably about change and continual revision—I am frightened when I see young writers overwork and over-revise their plays before finishing them.

When I teach playwriting, every year I inevitably encounter a writer who effectively unweaves what they write as soon as they write it. I call this: "Penelope syndrome."

I've had students who write and write, revising while writing and erasing their thoughts before the ink is dry. Perfectionists are uniquely prone to this syndrome. I've had playwrights rewrite what they've written during a rehearsal process so completely that every plank of wood in the play is pulled up and replaced by another plank, until it's a completely different play by the end of rehearsal, and not in a good way.

Is the fear of finishing a play, or any work of art, akin to the fear of death, of being done?

To these young writers, I say: if you want to finish your tapestry, wait until you are done to revise. Do not weave and unweave as you go. Do not erase your lines.

Lesson from a cranky neighbor

My three kids were out playing with young neighbors on our street in Brooklyn. It was dusk, and they were all yelling their heads off, with joy. Collecting acorns, stirring dirt with sticks. A neighbor in his seventies leaned out of the second-story window of our building and yelled at the kids until his cheeks were pink. "Be quiet, be quiet!" He added something for good measure about entitled parents who pay no attention to their own children. Then he slammed the window shut. The kids stopped playing, scared. They poured their acorns back into the dirt and went inside.

In the elevator, the kids cowered, saying they were scared to run into the neighbor who yelled at them. I knew this neighbor not at all, but I did know his wife a little, and I liked her. I knew she'd worked in education, and I knew she was kind. I thought: *I don't want my kids to fear our neighbor.* Then I remembered a children's book we had, *Zen Ties*, in which an elderly neighbor is cranky with kids, and a large panda encourages the kids to bring the elderly woman food, and it turns out that the old woman is sick.

So, thinking of that parable, I realized I had some extra pie I'd already baked with the kids. I told my kids to deliver the man some pie so they would get over their fear of him. They said they were too scared. I said I'd come with them.

My neighbor opened the door, immediately embarrassed that he'd yelled at the children. My kids hid behind my legs. I apologized for the kids' noise and offered him the pie. It was a peach pie with pistachio crust. He was flustered and apologetic and said he didn't need pie. His wife appeared behind him and said hello.

I said, "Please, take the pie, eat some, it's good."

I added, "I want to show the kids that you're not scary."

Embarrassed, he took the pie. And then he smiled. And after that, he always talked gently to the kids when he saw them.

I learned five months later that the man had cancer. I learned that only because I saw him in the lobby with no hair, clearly undergoing chemotherapy. I have no doubt that he yelled at the kids not only because they were being noisy but also because he was in terrible pain.

He died six months later. After his death, I became friendly with his wife and their dog, a dachshund. Just the other day she put a bag of clementines on my front door with a little note. I have a feeling she did this because she saw that one of my plays got a bad review, though she was too tactful to mention it.

I peeled the clementines and popped them in my mouth, tasting the sweetness. Sometimes you have to go to your neighbor's door and knock.

Arthur Miller and Tony Kushner are tall

I was reading a feature the other day in the *New York Times* about Tony Kushner. It mentioned that Tony Kushner was tall, really the tallest American playwright since Arthur Miller. *Huh,* I thought. *I never see women playwrights lauded for height.* I've met Tony Kushner several times, and he is tall, though not freakishly tall, maybe a little over six feet? Okay, wait . . . let me not speculate—the internet tells me he's six foot two. Why does the internet know that? I type in: *How tall is Paula Vogel?* Nothing. I type in: *How tall was Arthur Miller?* Six foot three, I find out. I try: *How tall was Lorraine Hansberry?* Nothing. No information on the women writer's height.

Measures of height are factual and descriptive, but was there a larger, unstated point in that *New York Times* profile about literary stature? When we speak of a work of art, we might use words like towering, or reaching literary heights. I love Kushner's and Miller's towering works of art. Also, I am relatively short. And most women are shorter than Arthur Miller and Tony Kushner. And it made me wonder if there was a feature penned about a woman writer, would her height be mentioned, and if so, what meaning would get made about her literary stature?

There is one theory about literary influence that is Oedipal. In this theory, popularized by Harold Bloom in *The Anxiety of Influence* (and forgive my gross oversimplification), the literary sons try to vanquish their literary fathers, and grow, metaphorically, taller than them. What, I wonder, of the women writers? Do they also want to grow taller than their literary predecessors? Often, I find, women writers want the opposite—to pull their precursors out of the shadows and into the light.

I remember once being at a PEN America award ceremony where Edward Albee and I were there to present an award. I met Albee in the green room, and he asked me for help putting on his leather jacket before going onstage. Albee was then in his seventies and had recently been in a motorcycle accident, breaking his left shoulder. I carefully helped him on with his jacket, first the left side, then I went around to his right.

He barked at me, "I didn't say I needed help with the right shoulder!"

I apologized for my overreach.

We went onstage together, and Albee introduced me as the "pretty and young playwright" he'd just met. For a moment, as the lights shone down on us, I felt delighted that Edward Albee thought I was pretty despite my unrecovered facial paralysis, and that in my mid-thirties, he thought I looked young, but the delight quickly turned to confusion and irritation. The words *pretty* and *young* were diminutive, unserious, and had pointedly nothing to do with my work. Serious writers, in the old cultural imagination, are supposed to be rumpled, wrinkled, beyond vanity, and, perhaps, tall. If you are tall, you can look down on the world with a kind of omniscience. Like a big phallic gnarled tree.

The other night I had a dream about Arthur Miller. In the dream, I went to Miller and his wife Marilyn Monroe's dilapidated house by the sea in Connecticut, and the house was for sale. It was creaky, moldy, and about to fall over, but Miller had built it himself, so it was of great value. The house tilted this way and that, unsafe. A boat and a motorcycle hung on the ceiling. There was a vast collection of books, and I wanted to take one book in particular—it was *A Portrait of the Artist as a Young Man*, and on the flyleaf was a drawing by Miller of a house he wanted to build, which made the book priceless. The book was moldy from age and the sea, but I dusted it off and stole it.

I opened the book that I'd stolen; inside was a great secret about living and writing. The secret was that there are two types of people: those who get trained to play in an orchestra and those who don't; those who keep playing when they hit trouble and those who don't. I thought Miller was trying to teach me something about artistic duration. Then, suddenly, I was in the water with my family; we'd been dumped in the sea, and a wolf was also swimming in the water, which was alarming. I woke up, worried about the wolf.

What was the wolf? A reference to *Who's Afraid of Virginia Woolf*? Or a wolf at the door? What was the sea? What was the book with the secret to writing and life? Was I more prone to the anxiety of influence than I'd thought? Did I, in fact, want to demolish a literary ancestor, the tall Arthur Miller? Or did I just want to learn from him, steal from him—for him to teach me how to write from beyond the grave?

I was about to go into rehearsals for a play of mine called *Becky Nurse of Salem*. The play was my answer to Miller's *The Crucible*. Miller wrote *The Crucible* while he was still married to his first wife; he confessed in an article that John Proctor's attraction to Abigail Williams was based on his own fraught attraction to the much younger Marilyn Monroe. When I learned that, I thought, my God, our country's whole understanding of the Salem witch trials is based on Arthur Miller's attraction to Marilyn Monroe!

And yet, as critical as I felt about *The Crucible*'s historical inaccuracies, my dream life may have been telling me that, as much as I wanted to write up against Miller, I still had much to learn from him. I was stealing his book (apparently, a theme of mine), and I wanted him to teach me about plays with sound architecture in my dream life.

A play is a collection of words; it's also a blueprint, a house for actors to temporarily occupy—a kind of spirit house. These towering playwrights who came before me—Kushner, Miller, Albee—apparently my subconscious desires their wisdom without the domination of their height.

The sad neighbor

My kids and I play a game where, as we walk, we look for dogs and their owners who seem to match—either because of their faces, hair, fashion, or invisible spiritual qualities. One such match between dog and human was a tall ginger neighbor and his tall ginger dog who lived down our block in Brooklyn. The neighbor, his dog, and the super of their building used to stand outside at the same time every morning, the neighbor and the super exchanging pleasantries, the super often giving the dog a treat.

I could almost set my clock to this whole silent interaction, like a rehearsed dance. I'd walk out the door to school with my kids, and we'd see the trio: ginger dog, ginger dog owner, and the super, chatting. We didn't usually say hello, but we nodded every day. I felt some nameless loneliness from the dog owner, though I couldn't say why. The dog and his owner seemed remarkably close; the dog owner seemed proud and happy in the presence of his dog.

One day, my kids and I noticed that the dog had a large tumor on his side. The tumor got bigger and bigger, until it was about the size of a grapefruit. Still, every day the trio was out talking at precisely 8:30 a.m. Days later, the dog developed a limp. Still, they all appeared every day like clockwork. Then one morning, only the super came out. My kids and I looked at one another—not good.

The next day, the dog owner, without his dog, and the super walked down the block together. I saw their backs receding. I imagined that it was too painful to stand and make small talk in their usual spot without the dog. It's easier, somehow, to make small talk with a dog standing between you. I thought this little walk was beautiful, and strangely intimate, a gesture of human kindness from the super to the bereaved dog owner.

The next day, the dog owner and the super stood again in their spot at 8:30 a.m. and chatted, again, without the dog. The dog owner took a little rubber ball out of his pocket and bounced it once, twice. Then he put the ball back in his pocket, looking very sad. What a melancholy replacement for a dog, that rubber ball. Maybe it belonged to the dog . . .

Later that day, I ran into the dog owner. I'd never spoken to him though I'd seen him every morning for about the last ten years while walking the kids to school. I felt out of practice talking to strangers after the pandemic. Our phones are now always at the ready to fill in silences when we are trapped with a stranger in an elevator.

But I got up my courage and said, "I'm sorry about your dog."

"Thank you," he said.

Then he said, "If I'm being honest, I'm a little lost without him."

We talked for a bit, about how large and inoperable the dog's tumor was, about how the man and his wife had talked about getting a new dog but decided against it; they couldn't bear to replace this particular beloved dog. For some reason I'd never imagined that the man had a wife; I'd never seen her before, and there was a completeness to the trio.

I said goodbye to the bereaved dog owner, and now, rather than nodding at each other, we always say hello when we pass. He still hasn't gotten a new dog.

Polly and the two-dollar-bill dream

I think dreams can be wonderful teachers. I try to write mine down, first thing in the morning. Sometimes dreams blur into my daily life in the oddest way. For instance, I was about to open my opera, *Eurydice,* at the Metropolitan Opera. I was overwhelmed, felt the need for old friends and comfortable high-heeled shoes—the latter being a total oxymoron. One of my oldest friends and collaborators, Polly Noonan, flew with my mother from Chicago to New York for the opera. Polly dropped my mom off at my apartment in Brooklyn, and I insisted on paying for the taxi, knowing that Polly's spiritual and artistic resources are unlimited, and that her economic resources are limited.

That night, I dreamed that Polly gave me two two-dollar bills for good luck on opening night, and she delivered a long soliloquy about labor and friendship. She explained in the dream that maybe money might seem like a weird gift to celebrate art, and maybe it was weird for an artist without a lot of money to give money away as a present. In the dream I told her that I understood the gift entirely and that art and friendship are so much more important than money. And in the dream, I happily took the two bills, and we continued to have a long dialogue in the dream about economics, labor, friendship, and art.

The next day I texted Polly that I dreamed she gave me two two-dollar bills. She texted back:

WHAT?!

She then texted me a photo of the two crisp two-dollar bills she was meaning to give me for good luck on opening night. She explained that she'd gone to the bank in Chicago, where she took out two crisp two-dollar bills for the occasion of my opera, wondering if it was a weird thing to give money as a present. I marveled at the dream and the two-dollar bills and said:

Message received!

I don't understand how the universe is built such that dreams can know things that we do not know in the daylight. I only know that my dreams are sometimes my best teachers.

Art is a dream we are allowed to have together; when we sleep, we dream alone.

On writer's block

When I was twenty, after losing my father, I had trouble writing. It was my teacher Paula Vogel who correctly diagnosed my reluctance to write a play; she knew that I was looking at the grief too directly. She taught me that I needed to look at the grief sideways in order to write. Sometimes we need a real live teacher, a voice who answers back, to see what we cannot see. Or to diagnose a very particular manifestation of what passes generally for writer's block.

I've since decided that writer's block is not real. It's an invention. A self-inflicted wound. A chimera. After all, every time we fall asleep, we write stories in our dreams.

When putting my children to sleep when they were little, I used to make up stories while we laid in bed together. We called this ritual "Boat of Dreams." I would tell them we were all getting in a little boat, paddling, and then I would make up a story of the journey. By the time we got to our destination, we were usually asleep. At night, with my kids, I never failed to make up a story, I never had a "block"; maybe because the stakes were high: *put a child to sleep*. Perhaps that is one cure for perceived writer's block— make your mission putting someone to sleep.

Whenever I give a talk to young writers, eventually a hand goes up asking about the phenomenon of writer's block and how to cure it. I think we should anatomize and rename the variations of perceived writer's block in order to deprive the term of its power. Another more apt phrase for what we call "writer's block" might be something more like "the studious avoidance of writing." It would be as though when I avoid exercise, I called it "exercise block." I have exercise block a lot. Almost every day. It's a real shame, but what can I do?

If I told a friend I had "exercise block," they might say, "You mean you're not exercising?"

"Yes," I would say.

Perhaps if a friend says they have writer's block, you might say: "You mean that you're not writing?"

"Yes."

I believe that the phenomenon many refer to as writer's block could fall into one of about twelve categories. The first is the aforementioned "avoidance of writing." The second is "waiting to write." Sometimes we do not want to work on a play or another work of art because we should be waiting until we know more, and the work of art comes to us. Perhaps this means we need to mourn for a while before writing. Or live a while more before writing. In any case, the art might be telling us that we should wait. A natural process, like gestation, can't be rushed.

The third category of perceived writer's block I might call "walking away from the canvas." We might choose to take a break from writing because we're too close to the material; we have to step away from the canvas, as a painter does every so often, to see how it looks from a distance. If we are *avoiding* writing, or *taking a break* from writing, the writer has some choice in the matter, whereas "writer's block" sounds like a mystical illness, like a gastrointestinal problem.

Sometimes when my students say they are having writer's block, I ask them what landscape they prefer: water, mountains, or meadows, and I tell them to get on the first train they can to the landscape they prefer, and to look at this landscape before trying to write again.

The fourth, perhaps most awful category, is "abandoning a piece of writing that should not be finished." This is a hard category, but occasionally a piece is not worth being written and should be abandoned. This is not mystical but a naturally occurring, and difficult to cope with, phenomenon. After all, one in four pregnancies naturally results in miscarriage, though people don't often acknowledge how common this is.

The fifth category is "I don't want to write the thing someone else is telling me to write." Or "I don't wish to implement the stupid notes on my writing someone else is giving me." This is a particular problem for writers-for-hire or graduate students and does not apply to the vast majority of writers. But this is not writer's block. This is revulsion, pure and simple. This is resistance to doing someone else's bidding. If the writer in this case is a person of means or already has an advanced degree, they can abandon the project and its attendant notes. If not, one must swallow, buck up, and *get it done.* Or explain patiently and tactfully to the person giving the notes that they are killing your soul. If you need to keep the writing job, take a mistress. That is to say, start a project that is yours and yours alone, a secret, nothing dutiful. Cheat on your paid work by spending time with your mistress.

The sixth category is "If I write what I would like to write, a person I love will be angry with me, or their feelings will be hurt." This applies to a large swath of confessional memoirs, revenge plays, and poems about ex-lovers. In many cases, this work should be abandoned anyway, because, as Elizabeth Bishop once said, "Art is just not worth that much." If the piece is worthwhile, however, one might get permission from the ex-lover, or mother, or grandfather before writing it. Or try a shift in intention, writing from love rather than from derision, and see how quickly the writing comes. That requires forgiveness, and forgiveness often requires waiting.

The seventh, unfortunately very common category, is "distracted by the modern world." If this sounds like you, turn off your phone or put it in the mail and mail it to yourself as my friend Jorge Cortiñas sometimes does when he's working on a project. It takes about a week for his phone to reach him again. If you find you're still distracted by the modern world while your phone is off or in the mail, you might need a more radical, ancient approach: meditation. Meditation, for the brain, is the equivalent of turning off your computer and finding it fixed mysteriously when you turn it back on again. Go on a silent retreat! Or, ride the Amtrak quiet car, the last place in the modern world where a conductor tells people that "a library-like atmosphere must be maintained." There are not even library-like atmospheres at most libraries anymore.

An eighth category for those with children: "I am distracted by my children." My prescription is to write outside the house if possible. The other cure I myself tried for this was writing in short form; micro-essays and haiku. Once the children are five and go to school for six hours a day, the problem naturally resolves itself, as one can really only write for two hours anyway (see the last category, general sloth).

The ninth category is "the beginning was not really the beginning, the middle was not the middle, and the end was not the end." There are at least two routes for every destination, as I tell my older daughter, who often only knows one way of walking somewhere. Sometimes we feel "blocked" because we started or ended a story in the wrong place. I find it useful for this condition to take a few months off between writing the first and the second act of a play. A corollary to "the beginning was not really the beginning" is "there are too many plays in my play"; in this instance, one might be liberated to write new scenes once the offending extra material is cut off. It's like being bloated and needing to fast before eating again.

Ten: the "Who is looking over your shoulder while you are writing?" syndrome. In this form of blockage, there is an overly critical parent, visible or ghosting, or an old teacher, or reviewer watching you write and waiting for you to write something stupid down. You might even feel that the culture you find yourself in (the culture itself!) is looking over your shoulder in a smug critical way. Prescription: do not look over your shoulder while writing. Write for yourself. Or think of a person you would like to give a gift to and write for them. I think many forms of perceived writer's block fall into this category and because it is so painful and personal, we try to make it mystical, and blame it on the act of writing.

Eleven: "I can't write what I'm writing because I'm not qualified, or I'm writing outside of my identity." This worry has come to me from so many students, and I tell them that I imagine a kind of triangle when dreaming up a character. When inventing a world, or a person, we can rely on: (1) imagination or empathy, (2) learning or research, and (3) experience or memory. If we are lacking one part of that triangle, we have to rely more heavily on another part, or we get a little wobbly. For example, if we don't have the same life experience, gender, ethnicity, or sexuality that our imaginary character has, we better make sure we use our imagination, empathy, and learning even more deeply so that we achieve balance. After all, we never have the *exact* same life experience as a character we dream up. Even in a memoir, we embellish; we have to imagine what other people were feeling in scenes that we ourselves lived through. Our life experience takes us only so far—imagination, empathy, and learning, I believe, must do the rest.

The last and twelfth category is general sloth. For "sloth disguised as writer's block," I recommend: caffeine, walking, deadlines, regular writing habits, cleaning rituals, jumping on a trampoline placed near the desk, and sleep. Tea should be used for certain writerly modes, and coffee for others. No need to resort to speed or cocaine, as many television writers have done when on deadline. Green tea is good for some temperaments and genres, but I find Yorkshire tea to be the best for me. Short walks with animals cure many writerly problems; long walks alone by the sea cure others.

Another prescription: limit the duration of daily writing. I don't know many writers who can write well for more than two hours a day. Maybe that's because I know more playwrights and poets than novelists, who have more stamina. If you try to write three hours a day and find you cannot, you might start by trying to write an hour a day, maximum. Find out what time of day you are most awake and write then. Many mystics and meditators find that 4:00 a.m. is a time of bold inspiration. I myself find the boring interval between 10:00 a.m. and noon to be fruitful. Ann Patchett has a useful trick, advising writers to sign into their desk, writing down on the sign-in sheet how long they spent there. When people do this, she says, eventually they do their writing, as if by magic. Another cure for the avoidance/sloth malady: find other writers in the same pickle and create deadlines for one another. You can bat away perceived writer's block and the professional hazard of loneliness in one fell swoop. I myself have my very own pickle council—four playwright friends who meet regularly, share work, and discuss professional pickles.

For sloth, I also recommend vigorous cleaning: by cleaning a desk, workspace, or theater, not only are you saying—I am responsible to this space—I take ownership over this space—you are also saying, with humility—I am not above getting on my hands and knees to clean a floor. You are saying, with your whole body, in case your body forgot where it was—I am here. There is a job in Tibetan monasteries called "the sweeper" for a young monk, and every day this monk simply sweeps. The theater has all kinds of rituals to remind us, in the words of Ram Dass: *Be Here Now.* Cleaning is one of them.

Nilo Cruz (brilliant author of *Anna in the Tropics*) was my teacher in graduate school, and he often had us get on our hands and knees to clean the theater space before we worked in it. He said that cleaning the space together was a way to show the space respect, and to take ownership over it. *A borrowed space is only yours if you clean it first.* You can always tell the state of my work life from the state of my desk. When I am just about to embark on a project, everything is thoroughly clean and in place; when I am mid-project, I allow the desk to be a mess—peels of clementines, papers, a couple of discarded almonds, spent tea bags—all attesting to the messiness of process. But when I finish a project and am ready to start the next one, I clean again.

Another general cure—sleep. Sleep is the most wonderful cure for any kind of writer's block, because of dreams, which remind us that stories make themselves up, if we only let them. It is useful to have a place for sleep near one's desk. When a form of dropsy hits while writing, we should pay attention and heed the horizontal impulse. Often a dream will come that gives us the next sentence, image, or event.

Now, say you have tried everything. You have anatomized your perceived writer's block, you've signed into your desk, you've tried tea, walks, waiting, forgiveness, the Amtrak quiet car, and nothing is working. Some *last resort* ideas. First, a change of place. The most radical version of which is: go to a country where people are speaking a different language. This is sure to create the desire to write in your own language in an entirely new way. That cure requires time and means, so is not very practical. More practical: simply go to a different coffee shop to write. A different library. A different *place*. Let the sounds of the new place teach you to hear differently as you write. Or: change the genre. Write the poem as a story, the play as a poem, the essay as a song.

If change of genre or country does not work, try the water cure: a bath is usually readily available. Or a nice long swim. Many of the most disciplined writers I know swim every day. Find joy in your body: dance, walk, run. Writing can be a disembodied activity, and sometimes the body requires joy before writing.

Finally, one mustn't confuse self-loathing or despair with writer's block. Those are professional hazards and there are other treatments for them. Please don't ignore them. And if none of the aforementioned remedies work, it might be time for you to find yourself a real live teacher.

A practical use of meditation

I was in Maine with my mother visiting a friend, sitting on the front porch, eating dinner. We were talking about, among other things, a family friend, a beloved Congregational minister, who had recently choked on a piece of steak at a restaurant. Though the Heimlich was administered, and the steak came out, she died in the hospital two days later.

We moved on to other topics, and I brought out pistachio cake. My mom took a bite of cake and suddenly started coughing uncontrollably. I looked at her, alarmed; she kept coughing; I ran into the house and brought her a glass of water. She had a sip, then started wheezing and spitting, and she grabbed a Kleenex from a pocket in her sweater and coughed into it. Was something caught in her throat? My mind raced; should I try the Heimlich maneuver, which I'd never done on an adult before? I flashed on the time my daughter Hope, then a baby, choked on a strawberry. I'd learned first aid while she was in the NICU, so I knew what to do: I'd immediately thrown her over my knee with her head facing down, and whacked that strawberry out of her mouth as her twin brother looked on, alarmed.

But on the porch in Maine, my mother was still able to cough, so I was dimly aware that the Heimlich wasn't called for, not yet. But suddenly she seemed to be choking and gasping all at the same time. Then she coughed up a small blue object. We all leaned forward and examined it. It was a small piece of yarn from her sweater, which had pilled and made its way into a Kleenex she'd used. She must have wheezed that little piece of yarn into her throat. We all relaxed. And my mom drank some water.

Relieved, I joked about how you worry all your life that some dreaded disease might kill you, not realizing you were going to get undone by your own lethal sweater. The killer sweater, we all said, laughing. But after the relief of laughter, my mother started coughing again. She stood up, and rapidly the coughs turned into a new set of even more terrifying wheezes. Suddenly she could not speak or catch her breath. My friend said, "She's turning blue." Sure enough, my mother was turning the shade of a blueberry. I'd been hoping I was imagining the blue color creeping into my mother's face, but seeing the look of panic on my friend Robyn's face, I yelled for a doctor, knowing full well that in rural Maine there would be none running over to save us. Was it time for the Heimlich, CPR, 911, or all three? Time seemed to stop as my mother's face turned purple and she gasped for air.

I tried to calm my mind and breathe. I hadn't done a CPR course in thirteen years and I didn't trust myself to do chest compressions. My mother was panicking. All I had at my disposal was my training in meditation, and I tried to find a little sea of calm under the rising tide of panic and remember what my meditation teacher, William Duprey, had taught me. "Mom," I said, putting my hand on her back. "Try to focus on your out breath instead of your in breath. Try to make your exhale long. If you can just exhale it will relax your breathing. Just one long breath out." Miraculously, she heard me, and started to focus on her exhale rather than on gasping for an inhale that was hard to find. My mother's wheezing calmed. The purple started to drain from her face. She was taking in oxygen. Her face turned pink again.

What would I have done if my mother hadn't started breathing again on that porch in Maine? I had once written a play in which a character dies laughing. Had my joking about the lethal sweater made my mother laugh, which induced the second, more dangerous bronchial spasm? Had I almost killed my mother with a joke? When I took her to the ER for a chest X-ray after the episode, the doctor said that she could have died from lack of oxygen, but her lungs were now clear, no foreign object there. Thank God. And meditation.

Over the years, I've picked up various meditation techniques, including one from an actor friend, Ernest Abuba. He taught me the simple five-seven-five technique; you inhale, counting to five, then exhale counting to seven, and then inhale for five counts again. He taught me that exhaling for two seconds longer than inhaling relaxes your nervous system. I remember at the time thinking, *Wow, it's like the haiku in breath form—five/seven/five syllables.* Sometimes I like to teach a group of students this five-seven-five breathing technique, sit in meditation together for awhile, and then have everyone write haiku.

Five, seven, five, I think, *five, seven, five:*

A blue knit sweater
that almost killed my mother—
breathe out more than in.

Theater as a school of presence

I was recently speaking to a high school theater class, and I asked them what gave them hope for the future of theater, given that the field has been hit so hard economically by a pandemic, and by the dominance of binge-watching Netflix in isolation at home. These students told me that the only time they could truly focus, could truly *be* with others in a focused way, was when they were in theater class. Theater class was when they could feel and practice presence, that elixir of life; that well of possibility.

Our phones have made it nearly impossible to be fully present. When are our phones off? Not on the toilet. Under water, yes. In jail, yes. In church, maybe. On the Amtrak quiet car, hopefully. In baby carriages, not always. And in the theater—always. Unless someone in the audience forgot to turn the ringer off. But even so—in the theater, when phones ring, *it is still considered a violation.*

The more technological tools we have, the more presence seems just out of reach. I am on the hunt for sanctuaries of presence. Places where people make eye contact. Places where people know how to play. Imagine—that group of young people doesn't know how to be present except for in their theater classes. In the olden days when schools took attendance, pupils raised their hands and called out "present!" Now the kids are there but not there. Now the grown-ups are there but not there. If we are not there, how can we be with each other?

The US surgeon general released an advisory this year declaring loneliness a public health epidemic. "Given the significant health consequences of loneliness and isolation," Vivek H. Murthy wrote in his report, "we must prioritize building social connection the same way we have prioritized other critical public health issues such as tobacco, obesity, and substance use disorders."

There is a natural and time-tested cure for loneliness that has existed for over two thousand years: the theater. Given two joint crises—the loneliness epidemic and the economic implosion of the theater—I would like to offer a modest proposal, that is actually no joke: Why not give emergency funding to our theaters from public health coffers? We could treat theater as a proven method to stem the tide of crippling isolation in this country. Theater treats the malady of loneliness and the malady of not being able to be fully present.

During lockdown, I fretted and mourned for my profession. But at least I could write, unlike other theater practitioners whose vocation depends wholly on being in a room with other people. I felt sorry for actors, and for all of the deeply present directors stuck at home during the pandemic. I spoke to the director John Doyle on Zoom during lockdown, and he said he was constantly rearranging his living room chairs and didn't know why, until he realized it was his way of directing. Like great teachers in a classroom, great directors make deep presence in a rehearsal room possible by the quality of their listening and the power of their gaze. I remember working with the director Anne Bogart, who writes, "Listening is a basic ingredient of attention, and it can be learned and practiced. Listening is fueled by interest and curiosity. It is a discipline and an action in the world, and the results are nearly magical . . . To be heard, really heard by another person, is to be healed."

When collaborations based on that kind of ineffable presence go well, they glow in memory, like a road that appears to shimmer when it's hot outside. One of my favorite collaborators and deep channelers of presence is the director Les Waters. He and I do a minimal amount of talking *about* a script. Our collaboration is intensely in *relation* but not necessarily in conversation. I don't know how to explain that, only to say that Les does not waste words. He penetrates the mystery of a work, which often must be done in silence. And always with a sense of humor. As he watches the actors with an unerring eye, the actors seem almost magically to adjust to his presence. The actors' choices become more refined because of how they are being watched—with rigor, curiosity, and affection.

In physics, the observer effect describes how a phenomenon is affected by the act of observing. A rehearsal room is basically the logical extension of Heisenberg's notion that "we can no longer speak of the behavior of the particle independently of the process of observation."

The rehearsal room, by setting up a frame for the observed, creates a crucible where students can mainline presence. To be present, we create a sense of ritual time—the sense that an event takes place at only this place, and this time, and no other. The digital advances over the past twenty years (Zooming, streaming) have collapsed our ancient limits of time and space, encroaching on ritual time. The effect is disorienting. I can speak only for myself. I am infinitely distracted. *What am I paying attention to?* Yet theater is the ancient art of directing an audience's attention.

Of actors they love, audiences will say: what incredible stage *presence* they have. How to account for this sense of electric presence that some actors have? An actor with stage presence seems to be reacting in real time, not overly rehearsed. Great actors trick us with two paradoxes. They are very prepared while seeming spontaneous, and they are deeply aware of the audience while pretending not to be.

How is this accomplished—training or natural charisma or both? The word *charisma* comes from Latin through the Greek *kharis*, "a favor, or divine gift." The ability to be and seem spontaneous is a gift cultivated through repetition and practice. The word for *rehearsal* in French is simply *répétition.* Just as when we meditate (plunking our behinds on a cushion daily until a feeling of presence arrives) so we repeat gestures in the theater until they become automatic. The more automatic the actor's words and gestures are in the theater, paradoxically, the less wooden and more alive the actor seems. In a great actor's face, a light goes on when they are being watched. Presence is not a solitary activity in the theater; *being watched* produces and focuses presence. It has been scientifically proven that being in an audience together actually synchronizes our heartbeats.

For two years of a pandemic, we were trying to practice collective rituals from our own bedrooms. I felt like I was cupping my hands around an ancient art form, that theater was a religious sect that had gone underground, and I was holding this little candle, to pass it to the next generation, and the winds were terrible all around us, threatening to blow out the flame.

Can you be your own teacher?

I was once doing an interview with the theater critic Helen Shaw, who told me that she divided my plays into two sections: before and after I was a teacher.

Then Helen asked me, "Can you become your own teacher? Or do you always need a teacher?" I paused. At first, I thought—*Yes, of course you can become your own teacher!* And then I thought—*No, you can never become your own teacher! You always need a teacher!* Being your own teacher is like looking at your own face without the help of a mirror—you can't do it.

We lose honored teachers over the course of a lifetime and can never replace them. In a perfect world, we internalize these teachers and their teachings. But do we need to keep finding teachers throughout our lives? I think that we do.

In Plato's dialogue the *Meno*, Meno asks Socrates, "How will you enquire, Socrates, into that which you do not know? What will you put forth as the subject of enquiry? How will you ever know that this is the thing you did not know?" *How do we know what we don't know?* Socrates answers Meno's paradox with his theory of recollection: the idea that we've had numberless lifetimes, and the soul is immortal. So that when we think we might want to learn something, we are actually trying to recollect something we dimly knew before we were born, in another life.

Without getting into Plato's theory of recollection, I would argue that this gap between what we know and what we don't know requires a teacher, at least in this lifetime, to mediate between what is known and what is not known. There is a quote that is falsely attributed to the Tao Te Ching: "When the student is ready the teacher will appear. When the student is truly ready, the teacher will disappear." Like Mary Poppins arriving at just the right time, then knowing the right time to sail away on her umbrella, the family no longer needing her services. The saying is of questionable provenance, claimed by some to be Taoist, others to be Buddhist; still others ascribe it to Madame Blavatsky.

Regardless of who said it first, or who said it at all, I like the idea that the student finds a teacher when the student is ready. In one mystical interpretation, when the student achieves enough spiritual attainment, they bump into the perfect teacher. In another interpretation, the teacher was there all along; the student simply had to shift perspective to see the teacher who was already there.

But why does the teacher disappear when the student has absorbed the teachings, when the student has become the teacher? Don't teachers also need teachers? Just like analysts need analysts, or doctors need doctors?

When I began learning to meditate, I gravitated toward books. I bought way too many books about how to meditate and I read them all. Pema Chödrön, Thich Nhat Hanh, Jetsunma Tenzin Palmo, Thupten Jinpa, Sharon Salzberg, and on and on. It was easier to *read* about meditating than it was to actually meditate. Almost every book said that it's better to find a teacher than to read a book, that you need a living and breathing person—that you need feedback. I absorbed the idea that I needed a person to observe me and respond; in short, a teacher. But, ironically, I continued to buy more books about how to meditate, more books that told me to find a teacher.

What would it take for me to be convinced that I needed a real live meditation teacher, not only books about the subject? After the extraordinary coincidence of running into Khenpo Pema Wangdak in a train station and seeing his teacher's handwriting in my book, it seemed as though I was getting a message from the universe. Still, I did not formally seek out his teachings for another seven years. What finally convinced me to seek out the teachings of a real live teacher after dabbling in meditation for years? Two things.

One: writing a book about teachers, at the age of fifty. Writers can take such a long time for our intellect to open our hearts, for our bodies to tell things to our minds. As I wrote, I saw that on almost every page, I was proclaiming that a live person, a teacher, animates a lesson. None of the lessons I obtained were reducible to words on paper. All required presence.

The classic Tibetan Buddhist text, *The Words of My Perfect Teacher*, proclaims, "We can see for ourselves that nobody has ever developed the accomplishments belonging to the paths by means of their own ingenuity and prowess . . . when it comes to following the path leading to liberation . . . [without a teacher] we are as confused as a blind person wandering alone in the middle of a deserted plain." And yet, our culture *loves* stories about people depending on their own ingenuity, originality, and prowess.

Two: another message from the universe landed in my lap. I was on the phone in an Uber asking a friend if he could recommend any classic Buddhist texts about the relationships between teachers and students. He recommended a couple of books, and I got off the phone.

I then looked up at my driver's name tag. It was Tsewang Lama. (*Lama* means "teacher" in Tibetan.) I asked if he was Tibetan, he said yes, he was, and I said hello in Tibetan, and he asked how did I know any Tibetan, and I said I knew very little but I try to practice Tibetan Buddhism. He said that was funny because he was an ex-monk. He asked if I followed a teacher. I said not really. I told him that I had taken refuge with a wonderful teacher, an Englishwoman who founded a nunnery in Nepal, but I couldn't really study with her, as she lived in Nepal. I asked him why he wasn't a monk anymore. He said maybe his luck had run out. He told me that, in his life as a monk, he'd worked with a French-born monk named Matthieu Ricard. I had been reading Ricard's book *the day before*.

The universe was telling me to find a teacher. I signed up for a meditation class with Khenpo Pema Wangdak. My first official teaching from Khenpo Pema was on Zoom, of course. Because that is what we do post-pandemic. And what he said to our little group on that day was this:

> At the right time in a person's life or in a culture, the teachings
> will come. But in recognizing the teachings, one can be like
> a child in a supermarket. When I first got to New York, my
> teacher told me to buy milk in the supermarket. I looked
> everywhere for the milk, I couldn't find it—there was so much
> in the supermarket, it was overwhelming—the milk was right
> there, but I couldn't find it. You can walk by a temple every day
> on the way to work and never see it, and one day you notice it.

In classical Tibetan Buddhism, the contemplation of the teacher's face can be a vehicle to enlightenment, not only the teachings themselves but also the presence of the teacher. I can see why. When a face is sculpted by a lifetime of devotion, merit, practice, and kindness, the face speaks as beautifully as any book. The wrinkles are oceans of paragraphs that speak of compassion, patience, and suffering. The face's language is not cognitive but visceral.

When you decide to study with a teacher and not a book, there is a sense of planting a flag, committing. There is something decisive about having a person who you are responsible to, and who is responsive to you. You can vaguely earmark a book about a subject that interests you and put it away for six months on your bedside table, but you can't do that to a teacher. Finding a teacher requires commitment and understanding that you still have need of a teacher no matter your age requires humility.

To commit, rather than investigate, takes time; for me, it took about a decade. There is a principle in the Tibetan Buddhist tradition that if you treat your teacher as a Buddha, the more like the Buddha your teacher will be, and the more blessings from the teacher you will receive. This radical notion posits that it is not only the qualities of the teacher but the quality of devotion toward the teacher that creates a transformation in the student's mind.

There is also advice in the Buddhist tradition not to trust a teacher blindly but to see how they live, test out their teachings, and then decide, after careful observation, whether their teachings are beneficial. This is a very different view from the way I learned in Catholic Sunday school as a child. In classical Buddhist texts, the student is supposed to verify whether the teacher has had a good effect on your mind, and on the mind of other students. This can take a long time; you might observe the effects a teacher has on his students for years before deciding whether the effects are good.

I've always been suspicious of gurus, and even the word *guru*. I never liked the idea of blind devotion, or anything that smacks of cults. And there has been so much abuse caused by the idealization of a teacher who is protected by structural hierarchy. I dislike guru-like behavior, particularly in graduate writing programs where some teachers behave as if only they have access to the One Secret Elixir. That's one reason I teach the class Lessons from My Teachers—to undercut the notion that there is only one way into the writing process and only I have access to it.

I met a writer on a retreat recently, someone who also practices Tibetan Buddhism. She told me a story about her life falling apart. She had a strong desire to go on a pilgrimage to Tibet to Mount Kailash, a sacred place, to start over. She was afraid to take the trip, afraid of the physical stamina required, afraid she might die there.

Her teacher told her with perfect equanimity, "Well, you might die there, you might not die there. You'll die eventually, and anyway, it's a good place to die. Whatever arises for you there, that is the perfect teaching."

Whatever arises is the perfect teaching.

This thought astonished me. How can we practice being attentive students to the teachings unfolding at every moment all around us? Our own curiosity becomes the teacher; our own thoughts become the object of meditation. In Sanskrit, the word for teacher (*adhyāpana*) and the word for learning (*adhyayana*) have the same root. Perhaps the truly enlightened can be their own teachers. But for the rest of us, still swimming around in the mud looking for lotus flowers, we need to keep finding teachers over the course of our lifetime.

My mother and Peter Pan

My mother grew up playing the role of Peter Pan in her hometown of Davenport, Iowa, at the community theater. As a child, I gazed at framed photos of my mother wearing green tights and flying. One large photo hanging in my grandparents' house even had Mary Martin, the famed Broadway Peter Pan, with her arm around my beaming teenaged mother. Mary Martin had come through Iowa on a national tour, and the local paper set up a meeting between her and my mother—the local Peter Pan—in a fancy dressing room. My mother was so nervous that she forgot her script in Mary Martin's dressing room; Martin had it sent back, signed, along with a bouquet of flowers.

So in my young mind, Peter Pan was always conflated with my mother, who embodied the magic of theater. My mother has always had an ambivalent relationship with the word *grown-up*, and she's stayed young, in the sense of being playful, and very much alive, in the theater.

I have a large extended Irish Catholic family from Iowa that has always been my own private cradle of civilization, along the banks of the Mississippi River. There I spent every holiday, catching fireflies with my ten cousins, reading books all day while dipping greedy hands into a jar of homemade Chex party mix, rolling down grassy hills, lighting sparklers on Fourth of July, and eating ham at Christmas. I also spent my holidays in Iowa listening to extended family argue about politics, a kind of family sport. At some point, I grew up, refused to eat ham, and stopped arguing with the people I love about politics because it was too painful.

On the occasion of my mother turning seventy, I wanted to write a play for her. It seemed a fitting gift for a woman who had acted all her life. I interviewed her, and all of her siblings, and then wrote a play, using the answers that they gave me as a starting point. I asked them these four questions:

What is wrong with this country?

When did you learn there was no Santa Claus?

How do you feel about your birth order?

Is there an afterlife?

I finished the play, *For Peter Pan on Her 70th Birthday*, and gave it to my mother for her birthday.

After I finished a draft, I solicited notes from my aunt, uncles, and mother. We did a reading of the play in my mother's living room, with my mom playing herself.

Someone asked my mother, "Isn't it weird, playing yourself?"

"Not really," she said. Maybe when you've spent a lifetime in the theater playing other people, playing a version of yourself is a homecoming.

For Peter Pan on Her 70th Birthday was done in Louisville, Berkeley, and New York, with my mother's role played by veteran actress Kathy Chalfant, who, at the age of seventy, flew in green tights. My mother and my extended family came to the show, meeting the actors, their avatars, at the stage door. My sense of honor meant I could not, out of nepotism, ask for my mother to be cast in these first productions. But finally, my mother got to play herself in a production of the play at the Shattered Globe Theatre in Chicago. I thought the world might implode in the Borgesian sense when my mother played a version of my mother onstage. But it did not implode. For me, it got a little bigger. And I felt relieved, as though I'd finally paid an odd debt. The debt of my mother compromising some of her theatrical ambitions to raise her children.

When my mother turned eighty-two, my sister and I helped her move into an independent-living complex in Evanston, Illinois. She'd been having trouble walking for months, and was scheduled for knee-replacement surgery that fall. My sister, Kate, and I wanted to make sure that my mother didn't take a tumble in the meantime. Kate and I had to go through all the objects in my mother's apartment before she moved; our goal—to get rid of at least a third of her books, objects, and furniture so that she could fit into her new, smaller apartment.

As my sister and I went through all the cabinets, pulling out dusty kitchen implements (she hadn't cooked in a long time), my mother sat on a wooden chair in the kitchen pointing at things with her cane, saying, "Keep that." "Keep that." She pointed to a stack of about twenty recycled gelato containers, saying she needed them to discard her used diabetes needles.

"How about one starter gelato container?" asked my sister. The office was so full of books, wrapping paper, and filing cabinets that it was almost impossible to clear a path to turn on a lamp. When I did plug in a lamp, the cord shorted out and almost electrocuted me. I sat among objects, exhausted. And to make it worse, my own nostalgia made it hard for me to part with a broken teacup, or a crumpled lamp- shade that reminded me of my childhood. Overwhelmed, my sister and I enlisted the help of a woman who came highly recommended to help older people downsize. She used to be a cop. Her name: Mary McHugh O'Sullivan.

Mary McHugh O'Sullivan walked boldly and with purpose into my mother's apartment and I felt immediately that things would be all right. A fellow Irish Catholic by birth with short curly reddish hair, she gravi- tated to my mother's Peter Pan hat, which had pride of place on a table. Mary exclaimed, "Ah! Peter Pan! I was the test pilot for Peter Pan's flight at Regina Dominican high school! I was on crew!" Of course she was, and Regina Dominican was where my mom taught high school. Mary was tough, grew up as a tomboy, had a twinkle in her eye, a deep laugh, and ordered us all around, arms akimbo. As she started to help us discard and pack, she told us stories about being a woman on the police force back in the day.

"So, I get this nine-one-one call," she said. "And in our town, the fire department went to any emergency with the cops. So I get there, and all these guys are standing around this lady who was screaming bloody murder with a needle through her finger. She'd *sewn herself* to her own sewing machine by accident. She'd been sewing something heavy like burlap, and the needle got impaled in her finger.

"The fire department guys were like, 'We're gonna have to take her to the ER, but first we're going to have to saw the goddam sewing machine off her. Someone get me a chainsaw!'

"I was like, 'Guys, move, move, let me through, I know how a sewing machine works!' And I calmly say to the woman with a needle in her finger, 'Okay, you and I are going to do this together, on the count of three. I'm going to lift the bobbin, okay?'

"She nods, and I say, 'ONE, TWO' . . . and before she can think about it, on two, BOOM, I flip up the needle. And I lift her hand in the air, and she was like 'Thank God! Those guys would have still been there finding a chainsaw while I bled out!' "

Mary made us all laugh, and as we laughed, we started to let the unnecessary objects go. As we made pile after pile, we learned that Mary grew up a block away from us on 518 Central Street in Wilmette, even went to our same parish, St. Francis. She remembered my father in his role as Catholic lectern. We gossiped about old neighbors and kept sorting through relics. We found the letter that my father had written to the insurance company, asking why they would not reimburse him for the wig he used after chemotherapy. We found the jacket with dried paint covering the sleeves that he wore when he painted the house. We let go of that jacket, finally.

And there were so many *trays* to throw out. As I found tray upon tray, I imagined some phantom life of entertaining where people were constantly circulating small bits of food. Mary threatened to bring her holster next time my mom tried to keep another tray. We even found the ashes of the family dog. Twenty-five years later, she had not been laid to rest. We drove to our childhood house on Central Street and dumped the ashes of the family dog on the lawn, hoping the new owners didn't see us, hoping it wasn't illegal. The line of ashes on the lawn looked like the work of a Zamboni.

How strange, I thought, *this doppelgänger Peter Pan is now helping my family move my mother to her new home. And she is helping us all grow up.*

At last it is moving day, and Mary told my mother to put her feet up and stay out of the chaos of the move, to let us do it while she rested. But my mother was in her new apartment, looking everywhere for something, seeming a little lost, circling.

Mary said, "What are you looking for?"

Finally, my mother said, "I can't find my Peter Pan hat. Did it get lost in the move?"

"It's right here," my sister said, handing her the hat.

So my mother put on her green hat with the red feather.

My mother still did not want to grow up, even as, especially as, she was moving into a place with a bunch of old people. She needed a marker of the boy who never grew up, the boy who could fly, the boy who could pretend.

My hope, when I wrote the Peter Pan play for her, was that every time Peter Pan died in my play and the audience resurrected her by clapping, my mother would live forever.

Becoming a teacher

The night before I taught my first class at Yale School of Drama, twelve years ago, I had a dream. In the dream, my mentor, Paula Vogel, was sitting in class with me, and she was teaching and talking, and I couldn't speak. I was mute, terrified.

The dream was obvious to me—I had a fear of stepping into her shoes, of having to use my own words. On some level, I must have wondered whether I had anything to share that was separate from what she'd taught me. I'd started teaching at Yale because Paula needed a substitute teacher that semester. She was busy with a production on Broadway, and she needed time off. I had two toddlers and a preschooler at home, and I wasn't sure I could manage a commute from Brooklyn to New Haven, but I would do anything for Paula, so I said yes.

The first day of class, the students looked at me anxiously. I was not the teacher they had come to love and know and trust. At the time, I still had significant paralysis on one side of my face from Bell's palsy, and I felt compelled to tell them that if I looked stiff or frozen or disapproving, it wasn't what I was feeling on the inside. They understood. And it turned out that I loved teaching. I didn't even mind the commute; the quiet car on the Amtrak train was exactly the holy space I needed to empty my mind.

I think I only scared a student in that particular group one time, and it was due to my math skills. I had told one writer that her play was marvelous, that the only thing left to do was make some cuts. I explained that a poetry teacher of mine asked us to do word reductions as a percentage. I then told this playwright to do an 80 percent reduction of her play. But what I meant was, she should keep 80 percent of her play! She looked at me, stricken.

What did I say? I wondered.

I took her out to lunch a month later and she said, "God, I thought you hated my play."

"No!" I said. "What would ever have given you that idea?"

"You told me to cut eighty percent of it."

"Oh no!" I laughed. "I meant twenty! I'm bad at math!"

And we became friends over shared soup.

A lot of teachers have imposter syndrome at first, no matter how accomplished they are, no matter how long they've trained, or how many books they've read. They wonder if they have something truly useful to impart. Though I had some awards under my belt, those external forms of recognition are not actually qualifications for teaching—a deeply personal exchange in which you must be convinced you have something specific to give.

I came to love being in the classroom, and Paula realized she needed more time away from the classroom for her own writing. So I ended up staying, and staying, five years, then ten . . . then twelve . . . I was no longer a substitute teacher. I was a professor. It took me years of teaching to figure out how to create a synthesis of many teachings I'd absorbed, along with a lifetime of experience making plays and writing. It took me patience and time to feel limber and fluid as a teacher, and to realize that listening is just as important as speaking. I realized that the teacher who insists on hierarchy and the trappings of authority over and above the dignity and self-determination of the student is really just an insecure teacher.

Perhaps an alternate interpretation of the dream I had when I began teaching was that I already had everything I needed in the classroom—I had the teachings of my teacher; in fact, she was right there with me doing the teaching. Looking back, I was doing a great job teaching in the dream, because I was listening.

I remember when I was twenty-two, wanting to give Paula a gift when I left college. What on earth could I give her, I wondered, this teacher who had already given me so much? Who had helped me find my compass, direction, and confidence? I ended up giving her the collected prose of Elizabeth Bishop. In that collection was a piece called "Efforts of Affection: A Memoir of Marianne Moore." Moore had been Bishop's lifelong friend and mentor, and Bishop writes of her very first meeting with Moore: "I was to find Miss Moore seated on the bench at the right of the door leading to the reading room of the New York Public Library . . . I learned later that if Miss Moore really expected *not* to like would-be acquaintances, she arranged to meet them at the information booth in Grand Central Station—no place to sit down, and, if necessary, an instant getaway was possible."

Their friendship was immediate and of long duration. So long, in fact, that when Bishop published "Efforts of Affection," Moore had counseled her to drop the original "and" ("Efforts and Affection") and make it "of." Bishop would later write the famous poem about Moore, "Invitation to Miss Marianne Moore": "Over the Brooklyn Bridge, on this fine morning, please come flying."

And when I feel despair for the world, for the passing of sages, I can well imagine thinking of so many of my teachers, the melody of that phrase: "Over the Brooklyn Bridge . . . please come flying."

I think that the best teachers secretly choose to keep teaching because they want to learn their whole lives long—and they know teaching is their best chance of learning. I hope to continue to orient myself as a student in this world. I have found that the older I get, when I find myself in dicey, irritating situations, my mind becomes more calm and supple, when I think of these two questions: *What am I teaching right now?* Or: *What am I learning right now?* One's attitude toward almost any situation can make it an occasion for a teaching, or a learning.

It is fall again. I have always loved fall, because the air becomes crisp, and it's time for school to begin. I get on the train from New York City to New Haven and find a seat on the highly prized quiet car. The quiet car, the only place I could write when my twins were little and they shoved each other off my lap, unwilling to share me. The same train where I once ran into a monk who became one of my teachers. The same train from which I wrote to my student Max when he was undergoing clinical trials, to distract him from nausea. I told Max that the quiet car felt like a kind of afterlife, and he wondered if the afterlife conductor would be a reticent beautiful Steve Jobs, handing out bread rolls. Today on the quiet car, the conductor's first name is Soul.

I am on my way to teach a workshop on reading and writing for joy and pleasure.

I always teach what I want to learn. I tell my students that there is no secret to writing well—but it helps to read well and widely. Sitting close to my teacher's teachings as I wrote this book reminded me to enjoy the practice of labor rather than the fruits of labor. Reminded me that inquiry is the thing itself. And when I've had doubts about my ability to endure the slings and arrows of a writer's life, its solitude and its discipline, the wisdom of my teachers has continued to give me ballast. And so a list of reasons to keep writing:

- Write for God. The cave. The envelope.
- Write for your mother. Your father. Your friend who is sick.
- Write for the future. Write for the past. Write for the present, but sideways.
- Write for the theatergoing politicians.
- Write for the ancient ones who go to the theater and immediately slip into a deep sleep.

- Write for the critics who haven't even been born.
- Write for the child who saw cruelty.
- Write for those dispossessed of language.
- Write for the actors who paint houses so they can still be in plays.
- Write for your daughter. Write for your son.
- If they don't exist write for the dream of them.
- Write for your uncle to weep, for your aunt to laugh.
- Write for your babysitter to cover her face with recognition.
- Write for the taxi driver who dropped you at the theater in Louisville and then accompanied you to the show.
- Write for the accountants whose eyes are too tired at night for numbers.
- Write for the farmers who grew your corn.
- Write for all the retired librarians like Pat Watkins from Madison, Wisconsin, who once wrote you a letter about your play.
- Write to thank the books you love.
- Write for the church you walked past with a sign that read: THEATER AT SACRAMENT. And you misread it as: THEATER AS SACRAMENT.
- Write for your teachers. Write for every single hour they left off writing their own sentences so that they could read yours.
- Write for yourself.
- Write for God. The cave. And the envelope.
- And when you are not writing for the inward, for the cave, for the envelope:
  Write for each other.

Epilogue, or how I wrote this book

As I wrote this book, I never failed to have an interesting conversation when I asked a friend or acquaintance, "Who was your most important teacher?" I learned about influential, lifesaving neighbors, bandleaders, martial arts teachers. I also learned who in my circle felt they never had a mentor. I learned who feared authority and who felt that they'd never been brave enough to ask for mentorship, to make themselves vulnerable in that way. It made me realize that finding a teacher is also a process of letting oneself be taught—which is a kind of bravery.

The process of writing this book was also a process of sending what I wrote to all the teachers I wrote about, the ones who are still living. Every essay I wrote about every person, I sent to them. Many of those people I regularly speak to, and others I had to track down after a long period of being out of touch. The essay about my piano teacher reached her, it turned out, on her birthday. I hadn't spoken to her in years. She told me she was so happy to receive it on her birthday, an unexpected present, and she also wrote me that she never really knows if she affects the lives of her students. I was shocked. It seemed so clear to me, the profound effect she'd had on hundreds of students; I couldn't believe that wasn't plain to her. And then it struck me—students leave, we fly the coop, and often don't report back. We might dream of the piano, but we don't send accounts of our dreams to our teachers.

I read a version of my essay for Tina Howe out loud for her at an event celebrating her body of work while she was still alive. Because of her Alzheimer's progression, she sometimes forgot what a vast body of work she had. At that event, droves of her former students turned out, and all her published books lay piled before her on a table.

"I wrote all these books?" Tina said, marveling. "Can I *have* them?"

Someone nodded, and she scooped the books up in her arms, cradling them and beaming. Five months later, she would be dead, reminding me that sometimes the window of time we have to express our gratitude is shorter than we might think.

While working on this book, I found myself ransacking my desk to find my professor David Konstan's old letters to me, written when I was taking a semester off, in mourning for my father. I thought the letters were tucked away in my desk, but I couldn't find them anywhere. So, on May 3, to hear his voice, I picked up his latest book, a book on the history of forgiveness, and started reading. A month later, I went to Brown University to accept an honorary doctorate at commencement. Another beloved classics professor from my undergraduate days, Joseph Pucci, conferred my diploma. Before walking out onstage, Joe Pucci told me that David had died of prostate cancer. On May 2. The day before I was ransacking my desk searching for his letters. Why did I not write him that May, or pick up the goddam phone, telling David I was thinking of him? Some spider sense told me to think of him around the time of his death, but no spider sense rushed in to tell me to call him, to write him, the week before. Why is it that lesson has to be relearned over and over again? I was glad that I'd at least sent him my essay about him months before.

Sometimes we forget to thank people whose addresses we have lost, but we also forget to thank people with whom we are still in proximity. My third-grade teacher, for example—Ms. Boland—became a close family friend. She and my mother still meet once a week for lunch. Ms. Boland was always kind, calm, and graceful, the kind of teacher every student wants to have. She had silver hair in a pixie cut, and she would run her manicured hands along the overhead projector and a sense of preternatural calm would come over me. When I was in her class, I decided that third grade really must be the best grade to teach, and that's what I wanted to teach when I grew up. Maybe I just wanted to *be* her when I grew up.

Not long ago, I went to lunch with Ms. Boland—Meg—and my mother, and we started talking about our old principal, Paul Nilsen. I wanted to be sure I had my story about him straight. Then Meg pulled a photo out of an envelope. There I was beaming on her lawn next to four other freckle-faced kids; I remembered the scene well. The winners of a reading competition were invited to the teacher's house at the end of the year for a party. This was *coveted*. To see a teacher's *house*? Holy of holies. Meg, now over eighty years old, had forgotten the names of two of the five children pictured, and I looked at the photo and reconstructed the names, which she wrote down carefully on the back of the photo, in her beautiful handwriting.

Then Meg took a note from her wallet to show me. A former student had written her the note after he was grown up, full of appreciation for how she had guided and nurtured him in the third grade when his parents went through a divorce. Meg said she never spoke to the student about the divorce, she just kept an extra eye on him. And this story reminds me that we can never codify an experienced teacher's intuition. The quality of her attention, presence, and listening, not a direct formal teaching, was what got this child through. One of my friends, a brilliant elementary school teacher, Sarah Curtis, told me that teachers must "teach everything, at all times." What she meant was that it was not enough to read a book to the kids on the rug, but you also had to teach them *how* to come *sit* on the rug. Teachers are constantly modeling implicit and explicit behaviors.

The way my third-grade teacher treasured this letter from her student reminded me of how rare it is for teachers to hear gratitude from their students later in life. So often, we absorb teachers in our minds, just as we absorb our childhood. They become *ours*, bizarrely disembodied, not people to whom we might write a letter, or bring a gift. But I did send Ms. Boland this essay and, while she was having an uncomfortable medical procedure, she quickly corrected some of my grammar and spelling, and reminded me that she was always Ms., never Mrs.; even though she was married, she'd never changed her name. How on earth could I forget? The first legendary Ms. I'd ever met.

I mention this part of writing the book because it takes quantifiably so little time to send a letter to a teacher, yet the benefits are perhaps unquantifiable. And the time taken to visit a former teacher is as helpful to the former student as it is to the teacher, I promise. In an age when we seem to be attached to our devices, when information is prized more highly than wisdom, one small cure is to spend time with people who lived through another epoch, who are better equipped to sit with time, and with each other, who seem to know better than my generation knows: how to *be*. While I wrote this book, sitting with former teachers was a balm.

As I write the words *former teachers*, I realize that I don't believe in that arrangement of words at all. There are no former teachers, not really. Teachers—the ones who truly taught you—don't stop teaching you, even after you leave their classroom. Teaching, over time, is ultimately unbounded by the classroom. Just as love is unbounded by time.

Acknowledgments

When I read over this book for edits, what most struck me was my absurd and bountiful luck to have had so many transformative teachers. Thanks to my teachers from preschool on up: Mrs. Anne (preschool); Mrs. MacGregor (kindergarten and first grade); Mrs. Tachau (second grade); Ms. Boland (third grade and beyond); Mr. Spangenberger (fourth grade); Mr. Kemp (fifth grade); Mr. Artabasy (the only junior high teacher I ever liked); Caroline Erbman (genius French teacher in high school and my guide to French feminism); Raissa Landor (brilliant high school Great Books teacher, introduced me to Virginia Woolf); Blossom Marmel (freshman high school history class, hardest grader, best name); Larry Rehage (junior year English in high school, introduced me to women writers of the Harlem Renaissance); Jack Maddox (junior-year history teacher, high school, introduced me to Leslie Marmon Silko and revisionist history); Beverly Baker (creative writing teacher in high school); Eloise Fink (poetry teacher); Jane Schwalbach (the *Odyssey* freshman year). In my play *Stage Kiss*, I wanted to put the names of my high school teachers in lights, and so I did. I dubbed them the coauthors of the terrible 1930s chestnut play within the play, and then I called for those names to be on a billboard in lights—Landor, Schwalbach, and Marmel.

A huge debt of gratitude to Joseph Pucci (all things lyrical and lovely; in freshman year at college, he taught the courses Ideas of Self and Dreams, Love and Confession, and introduced me to Sappho, Catullus, Horace, Boethius, Virgil. I tried to learn Latin from him too). To Coppelia Kahn (unparalleled Shakespeare teacher), Keith Waldrop (oh, this poet!), Ellen Rooney (introduced me to Tillie Olsen, Alice Walker, and Cherrie Moraga), David Savran (introduced me to contemporary playwrights), Mac Wellman (for his brilliant rants), Tamar Katz (the modernists), Tom Paulin (Elizabeth Bishop), Francis O'Gorman (Daniel Deronda and Yeats's dance plays), Victor Caston (Plato). To the friends I was learning with, and from each other—Jill Dawsey, Denise Milstein, Kirsten Deluca, Edan Dekel, James Platt, and Justine Malle. Of course thanks to the teachers already written about in the book: Nilo Cruz, David Konstan, Anne Bogart, Les Waters, Paula Vogel, Anne Sterling. And to many others who have had a deep impact, like Jessica Thebus and Ken Prestininzi, and so many playwriting colleagues who have taught me so much, too many to mention.

To my amazing students, among them: Max Ritvo, Erik Sirakian, Bonnie Antosh, Rachel Kauder Nalebuff, Phillip Howze, Brendan Pelsue, Emily Zemba, Tori Sampson, Mansa Ra, Molly Houlihan, Jeremy O. Harris, Noah Diaz, Majkin Holmquist, Alex Lubischer, Benjamin Benne, Kate Tarker, Mary Laws, Amelia Roper, Martyna Mayok, Genne Murphy, M. J. Kaufman, Jake Jeppson, Audley Puglisi, Margaret Douglas, and Jennifer June Buckley. In particular, thanks to the students whose list of things I learned in kindergarten I reprinted here: Esperanza Rosales Balcárcel, Rudi Cano, a. k. payne, Miranda Rose Hall, Matthew Chong, Emily Breeze, Doug Robinson, Andrew Rinçon, Comfort Katchy, Danielle Stagger, Stefani Kuo, Ida Cuttler. A special thanks to Esperanza for help with these galleys.

To my teachers in Buddhism and their teachers: Khenpo Pema, Jetsunma Tenzin Palmo, Mark Epstein, William Duprey, Yangzom, Sharon Salzberg, Gehlek Rimpoche, Thupten Jingpa, and Ghelek Rinpoche, and His Holiness the Dalai Lama. All sources of merit accumulated throughout past, present, and future, I dedicate to others, as have teachers before and after me.

To the doctors who finally diagnosed my Lyme disease—Dr. Patricia Coyle and Dr. Alfred Miller.

Thanks always and forever to Marysue Rucci, Dorian Karchmar, Emma Feiwel. Thanks to the writer's army now known as writer's shift.

Thanks to the frame game group: Emily, Steve, Tony.

And to Jim Shapiro and Paul Muldoon for all the lunches and conversations about writing.

And to the pickle council and early readers of these essays: Sarah Curtis, Erin Crowley, Polly Noonan, Andy Bragen, Crystal Finn, Kathleen Tolan, Julia Cho, Molly Gardiner, Sherry Mason, and Kathy Ruhl, of course.

For time and space, thank you to Ragdale Foundation and Hedgebrook.

Most importantly, thank you to my family for teaching me so much, Tony, Anna, William, Hope. Thank you for being patient with me while I get the words on paper, or when I'm looking into the middle distance thinking them up. I love you so.

Some of these essays appeared in other publications in different forms: *Poets & Writers, Double Bind: Women on Ambition, My Little Red Book*. One essay was adapted from an earlier essay I wrote in *100 Essays I Don't Have Time to Write*.

Permissions

A first version of "Lessons from Bleeding" was published in *Our Red Book: Intimate Histories of Periods, Growing & Changing*, edited by Rachel Kauder Nalebuff, Simon & Schuster, November 1, 2022.

*   *   *

First versions of "Dr. Seuss and Virginia Woolf, or Letter to My Daughters" and "For My First Teacher, My Mother" previously appeared in *Double Bind: Women on Ambition*, edited by Robin Romm, Liveright, February 27, 2018.

*   *   *

Earlier versions of "On Writer's Block" first appeared in *Poets & Writers* as "Writers Block: Variations on a Superstition," December 11, 2019, and "Not Writing Right now: Writer's Block During a Pandemic," May/June 2021.

*   *   *

A list of "reasons to keep writing" first appeared in a speech by the author to the 2020 Whiting award winners, published in *Vanity Fair*, March 25, 2020.

*   *   *

An earlier version of "A Lesson from Hope" first appeared as "The Four Humours" in *100 Essays I Don't Have Time to Write: On Umbrellas and Sword Fights, Parades and Dogs, Fire Alarms, Children and Theatre*, Farrar, Straus, and Giroux, September 2, 2014.

*   *   *

The essay called "Paula Vogel" has previously appeared in another version called "Is Playwriting Teachable?: The Example of Paula Vogel" in *100 Essays I Don't Have Time to Write: On Umbrellas and Sword Fights, Parades and Dogs, Fire Alarms, Children and Theatre*, Farrar, Straus, and Giroux, September 2, 2014; in the September/October 2009 issue of *The Dramatist*, and in *The Brown Reader* (Simon & Schuster, 2014).

About the Author

Sarah Ruhl is a playwright, essayist, and poet. Her fifteen plays include *In the Next Room (or The Vibrator Play)*, *The Clean House*, and *Eurydice*. She is a two-time Pulitzer Prize finalist, a Tony Award nominee, and the recipient of the MacArthur "Genius" Fellowship. Her books include *Smile: A Memoir* and *100 Essays I Don't Have Time to Write* (a New York Times Notable Book). For the past twelve years, she has been on the faculty at Yale School of Drama, and you can read more about her work at sarahruhlplaywright.com